UP TO YOU!

Anglais
A2-B1

2de BAC PRO

Ouvrage coordonné par **Corinne Tomasini**
IEN anglais-lettres, académie de Nancy-Metz

John Andrews
Professeur d'anglais au lycée général et technologique Fabert, Metz (57)

Patricia Bertolo
Professeure d'anglais-lettres au lycée professionnel Maryse Bastié, Hayange (57)

Véronique Bidon
Professeure d'anglais-lettres au lycée des métiers du bâtiment, Montigny-les-Metz (57)

Aline Idoux
Professeure d'anglais-lettres à la section d'enseignement professionnel Louis de Cormontaigne, Metz (57)

Ce manuel applique les rectifications orthographiques publiées par le *Journal officiel* de la République française le 6 décembre 1990.

DELAGRAVE

REMERCIEMENTS

Au cours de son élaboration, UP TO YOU! a bénéficié de nombreux conseils de la part d'enseignantes et d'enseignants d'anglais, de métropole et d'outre-mer.

Les éditions Delagrave les remercient vivement pour ce travail collaboratif.

- **Maud BESWICK,** MABLY, Loire (42)
- **Cristelle BRETON,** GRENOBLE, Isère (38)
- **Lorraine CHABANNES,** NICE, Alpes-Maritimes (06)
- **Claudie CORBETTA-NAVARRO,** MONTBARD, Côte-d'Or (21)
- **Sophie DESRIAUX,** ROUEN, Seine-Maritime (76)
- **Nathalie DUBOIS,** CHAMPCEVINEL, Dordogne (24)
- **Laureline DUQUENNE,** SARTROUVILLE, Yvelines (78)
- **Servane GEVEAUX,** CANNES, Alpes-Maritimes (06)
- **Claudia HERNANDEZ ALCALA,** MARSEILLE, Bouches-du-Rhône (13)
- **Nelly LE CORRE,** LORIENT, Morbihan (56)
- **Christelle MANZIN,** SAINT-BENOIT, La Réunion (974)
- **Sandrine MARTINELLI,** CONGIS-SUR-THEROUANNE, Seine-et-Marne (77)
- **Lucie MARY,** ALENÇON, Orne (61)
- **Lydie PAGET,** SAINT-PIERRE-DES-CORPS, Indre-et-Loire (37)
- **Florence PETIT-MABILLEAU,** ANGERS, Maine-et-Loire (49)
- **Laurence SMAGGHE,** LOOS, Nord (59)
- **Jacques VOITOT,** PONTARLIER, Doubs (25)

Et tous ceux dont nous n'avons pas pu recueillir les noms à temps.

ISBN : 9782206402413

5, allée de la 2e D.B. – 75015 Paris
editions-delagrave.fr

SOMMAIRE

SOMMAIRE

AUDIO
07 pistes audios
www.lienmini.fr/40241-45

Sur www.lienmini.fr/40241-45, retrouvez tous les documents sonores du manuel et les exercices de prononciation en accès direct.

PRÉSENTATION DE L'OUVRAGE

OUVERTURE DE L'UNITÉ

Une double page pour entrer dans l'unité :

- **Une photo** ancrée dans la vie quotidienne ou professionnelle
- ***YOUR ROAD MAP*** annonce le parcours de l'unité : **KEY QUESTION** comme fil conducteur, un **SCENARIO** pour s'immerger dans un univers anglophone, **deux ou trois tâches intermédiaires** pour préparer la **MISSION**
- ***Open up!*** pour entrer dans la thématique à partir d'un document sonore, iconographique ou vidéo
- ***Get ready!*** pour mobiliser le lexique en classe (**In-Class Activities**) ou en autonomie (**By yourself!**)

ROADS

Dans chaque unité, 2 ou 3 doubles pages d'activités :

- Un parcours différencié **LISTENING ROAD** ou **READING ROAD** pour développer des stratégies de compréhension à partir d'un support audio, visuel ou écrit
  - le parcours qui correspond au niveau visé
  - **Easy road** : un parcours numérique jalonné d'aides pour atteindre le même niveau de compréhension ou de production
  - **Extra road** : des activités complémentaires pour se dépasser et aller vers le bac (Vers le Bac)
  - des activités numériques complémentaires
- Une **TÂCHE INTERMÉDIAIRE** pour préparer la tâche finale
- Une page **Challenge yourself!** pour étudier la langue en contexte : culture, vocabulaire, grammaire, prononciation, verbes irréguliers
- Une rubrique **WHAT ABOUT YOU?** pour donner son avis et s'impliquer
- Une *citation* inspirante

PLAY WITH...

Une double page d'activités ludiques pour travailler et manipuler la langue :

- en autonomie ;
- à deux ;
- en groupe.

MISSION CONTROL

La mission finale avec :

- Un **guidage** détaillé
- Un rappel de la **KEY QUESTION** pour mesurer l'avancement des idées et se préparer à l'épreuve du bac
- Une rubrique **Assess Yourself** pour s'auto-évaluer

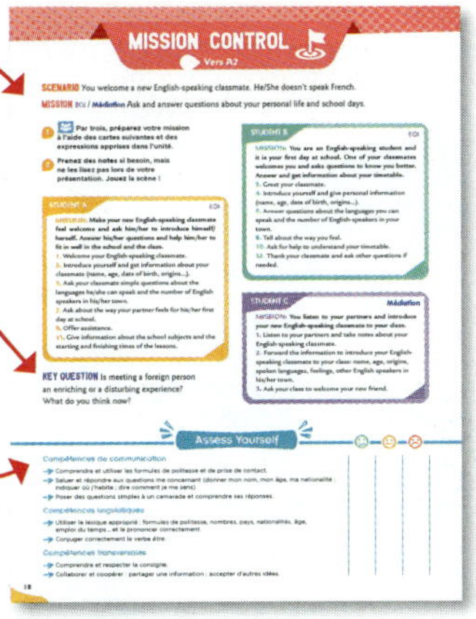

MICRO PROJECT OU EXAM ROAD

- Un **Micro Project** pour travailler en interdisciplinarité

OU

- Des **activités** pour se préparer progressivement aux épreuves du bac

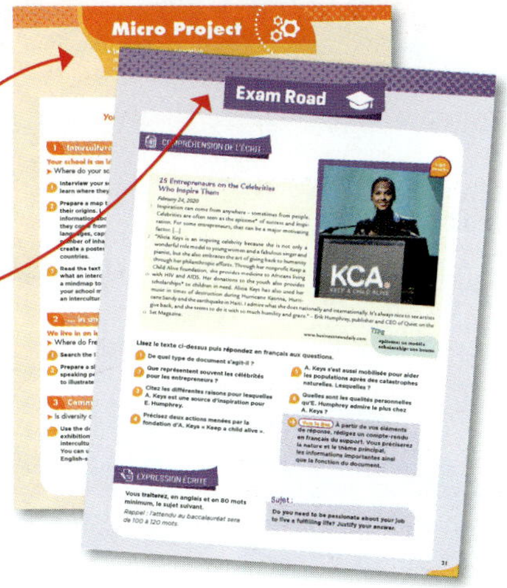

ACCOMPAGNER

- **Personnaliser** pour apprendre à apprendre, mettre en application les stratégies des fiches **Method & Strategies** et gagner en autonomie
- **Ouvrir, Orienter, Oser** pour s'ouvrir au monde, préparer son orientation et oser la mobilité
- **Consolider** pour revoir les notions étudiées

DES FICHES RESSOURCES

- **Method & Strategies** pour donner accès en autonomie aux stratégies de compréhension, production et interaction
- **Words** pour retrouver tout le vocabulaire rencontré dans les unités
- **Recap** : les fiches mémo des règles grammaticales et phonologiques découvertes dans les **Challenges**

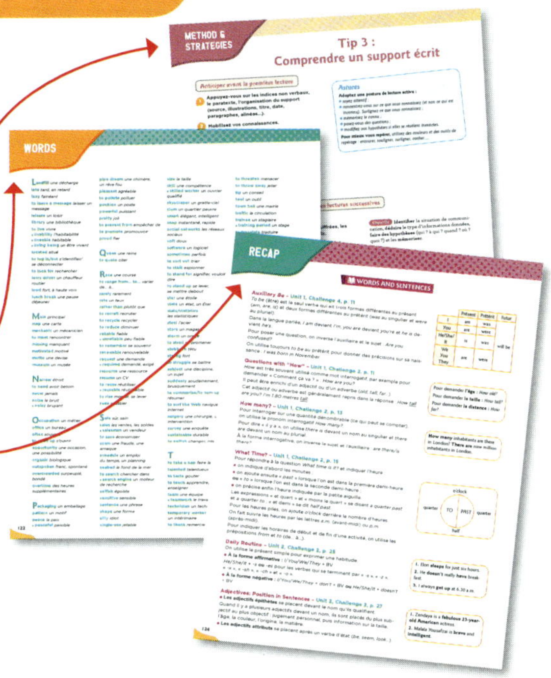

Bonus Road :

- **activités guidées** Easy Road ;
- **activités complémentaires** pour aller plus loin (challenges, sujets complets type bac, exercices supplémentaires…) ;
- **outils diagnostics** (tableau de suivi des compétences…).

UNIT 1

Vers A2

This

- Usages et règles de savoir-vivre
- École et vie scolaire
- Approche des métiers et qualifications

Look at the document. **Describe** what you see and what the young people are doing.

YOUR ROAD MAP

www.lienmini.fr/40241-01

UP TO YOU!

- Easy Road
- Extra Road
- Bonus Road

KEY QUESTION Is meeting a foreign person an enriching or a disturbing experience?

SCENARIO You welcome a new English-speaking classmate. He/She doesn't speak French.

TASK 1 SPEED MEETING **EOC** Give personal information (name, age, origin, qualities...).

TASK 2 CONVERSATION TIME **EOI** Ask and give information about nationalities.

TASK 3 OFFER HELP **EE** / ***Médiation*** Write a timetable and give information about it.

MISSION **EOI** / ***Médiation*** Ask and answer questions about your personal life and school days.

Is us!

Open up!

VIDEO
First Encounter with Pepper / 0'53
www.lienmini.fr/40241-02

1 **Watch** and **listen** to the video.

a. What sort of document is it?

b. How many persons can you see? How do they feel? Say as many things as you can about them (sex, age, nationality, language, feelings and reactions...).

2 **Listen again** carefully.

a. Find the two words used to greet people.

b. Find the two adjectives used to qualify the robot.

WHAT ABOUT YOU?

1 Do you know other expressions to greet and welcome people?

2 How would you feel in front of a humanoid robot?

Get ready!

In-Class Activities

EXERCICES
Flashcards
www.lienmini.fr/40241-03

1 **Look at** the flashcards, **listen to** the words and **repeat**.

2 **Memorise** the way the words are written.

3 **Link** the emoticons and the words.

a. silly   b. confused   c. puzzled   d. impressed
e. enthusiastic   f. bored   g. stressed

By yourself!

Think about films with robots. What are the robots' names?
What do you know about them?

Join us!

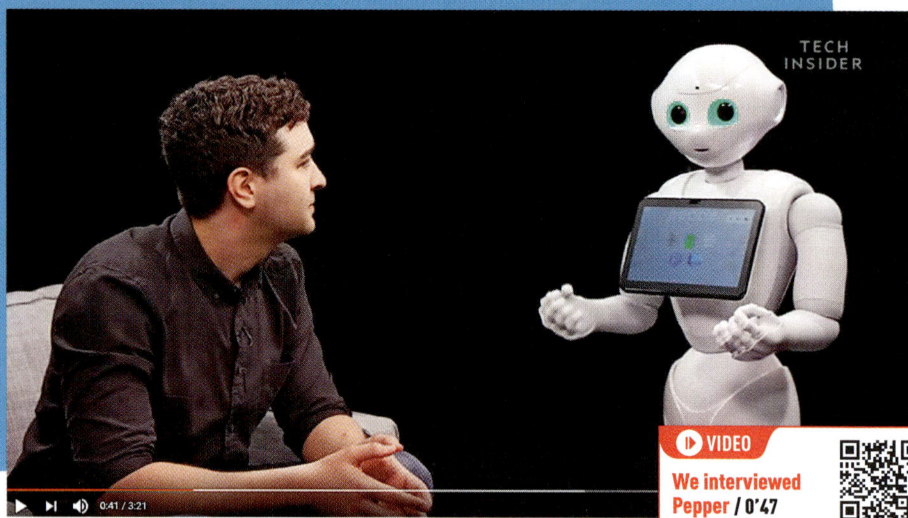

VIDEO
We interviewed Pepper / 0'47
www.lienmini.fr/40241-04

→ Method & Strategies
Tip 2 : Comprendre un support audio ou vidéo

1 **Look at** the above picture and the title. **Describe** what you see. Can you guess the subject of the video?

2 **Watch** and **listen to** the video. What sort of document is it? How many characters can you see? Are they in a noisy environment?

3 **Watch** the video **again** and **pay attention** to the names, the numbers, the places and the words you know. **Find out** as much information as you can about Pepper. **Discuss** with your classmates to summarise what you know about Pepper.

4 **Listen again** and **find** Pepper's answers to the interviewer's questions or sentences.
a. Tell me about yourself.
b. You come from Paris?
c. Why did they call you Pepper?
d. Do you have any feelings?
e. How old are you?
f. You're cute!

5 **Match the words (a) with their translation (b).**
a. to join – to help – to tell about – to keep on + *-ing* – to call – to remember – to translate – I was born in... – to understand – an answer – silly – to wave
b. aider – appeler – comprendre – continuer à – idiot – se joindre à – Je suis né à... – parler de – une réponse – saluer – se souvenir – traduire

Extra Road Vers le Bac

6 **Find the questions you could ask Pepper to get information about his name, age, origin, place of birth and height.**
Examples: Place of birth: Where were you born? Age: How old are you?

7 **Ask your neighbour these questions.**

WHAT ABOUT YOU?

Which other questions would you like to ask Pepper?

"Be yourself; everyone else is already taken."
Oscar Wilde

TASK 1

SPEED MEETING EOC Give personal information.
Pepper welcomes you at school. You have 1 minute to say as many things as you can about yourself.

Challenge yourself!

My Language Challenges	J'ai des difficultés ou je réponds non...
1. Je connais au moins 6 manières d'indiquer mes sentiments/mes réactions.	je fais le challenge n° 1.
2. Je suis capable de poser des questions sur les sensations, la taille, le poids, la distance.	je fais le challenge n° 2.
3. Je sais prononcer des questions ouvertes et des questions fermées avec la bonne intonation.	je fais le challenge n° 3.
4. Je sais conjuguer *to be* à toutes les personnes du présent, prétérit et futur à la forme affirmative.	je fais le challenge n° 4.

Challenge 4

Challenge 1 WORDS AND CULTURE Feelings and Reactions

1 Take up the challenge!

Classez les adjectifs suivants en 2 catégories selon qu'ils ont un sens positif ou un sens négatif, puis **traduisez**-les.

silly – confused – happy – stressed – angry – afraid – enthusiastic – excited – delighted – disappointed – sad – puzzled

2 Find the word!

Fermez les yeux et **donnez** 6 adjectifs que vous connaissez pour exprimer un sentiment, une réaction. **Vérifiez** vos réponses.

→ FLAP: Feelings and Reactions

Play with Words and Culture Memory Game

Challenge 2 WORDS AND SENTENCES Questions with *How*

1 Take up the challenge!

a. **Retrouvez** la question posée par le journaliste pour connaître l'âge de Pepper et **repérez** le mot interrogatif.

b. Quelle question le journaliste aurait-il pu poser à Pepper pour connaitre sa taille ?

c. Connaissez-vous d'autres questions qui commencent par ce même mot ?

2 Find the rule!

Le mot interrogatif ... signifie « comment » : « Comment vas-tu ? » : *How are you?*

Il peut être enrichi d'un adjectif ou d'un adverbe pour demander :

- l'âge : ... ;
- la taille : ... ;
- la distance : ... .

Cet adjectif ou adverbe est généralement repris dans la réponse : *How **old** are you? I'm 4 years **old**.*

RECAP > p. 124
Play with Words et Sentences n° 7

Challenge 3 WORDS AND SOUNDS *Wh-* or *Yes/No* Questions

1 Take up the challenge!

01 **Écoutez** ces questions. L'intonation est-elle montante ou descendante ? Pourquoi ?

2 Find the sound!

- En général, les questions ouvertes (*Wh- questions* = on attend un élément de réponse) ont une intonation ... .
- Les questions fermées (*Yes/No questions* = la réponse est « oui » ou « non ») ont une intonation ... .

RECAP > p. 127
Play with Words and Sounds n° 11

Irregular Session

02 **Retrouvez** les trois verbes irréguliers *speak*, *come* et *meet* dans le rabat à la fin du livre. **Écoutez**-les, **répétez**-les et **mémorisez**-les.

2. READING ROAD
Vers A2

Open your World!

Where Do all the English-Speaking Expats Live in France?

How many English-speaking folk live in France and where are they all? Here's what you need to know about where all the Australians, the Canadians, the Irish, the Brits, the Indians, the New Zealanders, the South Africans and Americans live in France. [...]

Stats given to *The Local* by France's statistics gods at INSEE reveal some interesting insights into the country's Anglophone population, which we narrowed down to Americans, British, Indians, Irish, Canadians, Australians, New Zealanders and South Africans. So apologies to those we left out. [...]

1. Total number

In all, according to INSEE there are 230,491 native English speakers in France and it won't surprise anyone who has been to Dordogneshire or even Charenteshire for that matter that Brits dominate the Anglophone population. Officially there are 151,767 *rosbifs*. There are likely many more who spend much of the year in France but are not officially residents.

In second place come Americans, of whom there are 31,000 in France. In third place are Indians, whose population totals 19,134 [...].

The Local, 16 May 2018

1 **Look at the illustration and find out common points and differences between the flags you can see. Which country do they belong to? Why are they on the French map?**

2 **Look at the text and choose the right answer.**

a. The document comes from: a novel / a press article.

b. It was written: in 2018 / in March / on 16 May 2008.

c. The numbers refer to the number of: English-speaking persons in France / people who come back to France every year.

3 **Read the text.**

a. **Look at** the questions at the beginning of the text. What sort of information will you find in the document?

b. **Point to** the words beginning with capital letters. What do they correspond to?

c. **Answer** the question: how many English-speaking people and how many Brits, Americans and Indians are there in France?

Extra Road — Vers le Bac

4 **Read the rest of the article and answer the questions.**

a. How many English speakers are there in Île-de-France? In Paris?

b. Is it astonishing? Why?

Quote the text.

→ **Method & Strategies**
Tip 3 : Comprendre un support écrit
→ **FLAP:** Question Words

WHAT ABOUT YOU?

Which languages can you speak?
Example: I can speak Spanish.
I'm a Spanish-speaker.

"You may say I'm a dreamer, but I'm not the only one."
John Lennon

DOCUMENT
Where do all the English-speaking expats live in France?
www.lienmini.fr/40241-05

TASK 2

CONVERSATION TIME EOI Ask and give information about nationalities.

Student A: You meet a new English-speaking classmate for the first time and you **ask** him/her about his/her origins and the number of English speakers in his/her district, his/her town.

Student B: **Answer** student A's questions.

Challenge yourself!

My Language Challenges	J'ai des difficultés ou je réponds non...
1. Je connais au moins 10 adjectifs de nationalité et je sais nommer les habitants d'un pays.	je fais le challenge n° 1.
2. Je suis capable de poser des questions sur une quantité et d'y répondre en utilisant l'expression « il y a » au singulier et au pluriel.	je fais le challenge n° 2.
3. Je sais prononcer les mots de deux syllabes et les adjectifs de nationalité.	je fais le challenge n° 3.
4. Je connais les nombres cardinaux jusqu'à 9 999, suis capable de les écrire et de les prononcer correctement.	je fais le challenge n° 4.

Challenge 4

Challenge 1 WORDS AND CULTURE Nationalities and Inhabitants

1 Take up the challenge!

Observez :

a. My friends are Austral<u>ian</u>.

b. ... where all <u>the</u> Australians live in France.

- **Repérez** les mots qui désignent les nationalités. Que remarquez-vous ?
- **Fermez** les yeux et **donnez** 10 adjectifs de nationalité.

3 Find the word!

- Les adjectifs de nationalité prennent toujours une ... . Comme tous les adjectifs, ils sont invariables.
- En général, on ajoute le déterminant ... devant l'adjectif de nationalité pour former le nom des habitants du pays. Mais il existe des exceptions.

→ FLAP: Nationalities

Play with Words and Culture n° 1 et 2

Challenge 2 WORDS AND SENTENCES How Many?

1 Take up the challenge!

Observez :

a. How many native English speakers are there?

b. There are 230,491 native English speakers in France.

c. There is a flag in the classroom.

- **Repérez** le mot interrogatif qui permet d'interroger sur le nombre et les expressions qui permettent de traduire « il y a » au singulier et au pluriel.
- Que se passe-t-il dans la question ?

2 Find the rule!

- Pour interroger sur une quantité dénombrable, on utilise le pronom interrogatif ... .
- Pour dire « il y a », on utilise ... devant un nom singulier et ... devant un nom pluriel.
- À la forme interrogative, on ... le sujet et l'auxiliaire : *is there...? / are there...?*

RECAP > p. 124
Play with Words and Sentences n° 8

Challenge 3 WORDS AND SOUNDS Saying Nationalities

1 Take up the challenge!

03 **Écoutez** ces adjectifs de nationalité et **tapez** dans vos mains au rythme de la syllabe accentuée (*exemple* : *Chi**nese**, A**me**rican, **En**glish*).

Répétez-les en gardant le même rythme.

2 Find the sound!

- En général, les mots de deux syllabes sont accentués sur la ... syllabe : *English, Spanish, Irish*.
- Les mots qui se terminent par le son **-*ese*** sont accentués sur la ... syllabe : *Chinese, Portuguese*.
- Les mots qui se terminent par le son **-*ian*** sont accentués sur l' ... syllabe : *Indian, Canadian, Australian*.

RECAP > p. 127
Play with Words and Sounds n° 12

Irregular Session

04 **Retrouvez** les trois verbes irréguliers ***find***, ***think*** et ***write*** dans le rabat à la fin du livre. **Écoutez**-les, **répétez**-les et **mémorisez**-les. **Révisez** les trois verbes appris précédemment.

School Is Cool!

Year 11 – School Timetable

Period	Monday	Tuesday	Wednesday	Thursday	Friday
8:30 am - 8:50 am	Assembly	Assembly	Assembly	Assembly	Assembly
Period 1 9:00 am - 9:50 am	Science S23	French L5	Maths S11	English L13	History L36
BREAK					
Period 2 10 am - 10:50 am	IT T7	Maths S11	IT T7	French L5	Science S23
BREAK					
Period 3 11:00 - 11:50	English L13	English L13	IT T7	Science S23	Science S23
LUNCH					
Period 4 12:30 am - 1:20 pm	PE	IT T7	English L13	Maths S11	Maths S11
BREAK					
Period 5 1:30 pm - 2:20 pm	PE	IT T7	History L36	IT T7	Maths S11
BREAK					
Period 6 2:30 pm - 3:20 pm	PLP	Unscheduled teachers available for one-to-one and group support	Unscheduled teachers available for one-to-one and group support	PLP	Unscheduled teachers available for one-to-one and group support
BREAK					
3:40 pm - 5:30 pm	Optional after-school club activity	Optional after-school club activity	Optional after-school club activity	Optional after-school club activity	Optional after-school club activity

HSDC* – Vocational Courses

TIP
HSDC: Havant & South Downs College
hands-on: pratique, « sur le terrain »

1 Increase your employability with a vocational course.

Vocational courses (often referred to as BTEC courses) are great if you're a hands-on* learner. They concentrate on teaching you the practical skills you need to successfully transition from education to full time employment.

HSDC has a wide variety of vocational courses, offering subjects ranging from Animal Care and Engineering, to Performing Arts and Public Services.

Our vocational courses are taught at both our Alton and South Downs campuses, where you'll have the opportunity to learn using industry standard equipment.

www.hsdc.ac.uk/study-with-us/vocational-courses/

CULTURE TOOLS
En Grande-Bretagne :
- Year 1 : dernière année de maternelle.
- Year 11 : Seconde.

1 **Look at** the title and the source of the text. What sort of document is it? What is it about?

2 **Read** the text. **List** all the words you understand, **find** the keywords and **choose** the right answer.
a. HSDC is a school teaching: various vocational subjects / scientific subjects / literature and languages.
b. The main goal of a vocational school is: to prepare students for university / to help students to find a summer job / to prepare students for professional life.

3 **Look at** the chart (see Annex p. 112).
a. What type of document is it? **Justify your answer.**
b. **List the school subjects you understand.** What are the missing subjects compared to your timetable?
c. **Guess what IT and PE stand for.**

→ Method & Strategies
Tip 3 : Comprendre un support écrit

4 **Look at** the times.
a. What time does the school day start/finish?
b. How long is a lesson?
c. **Complete the following sentence:** "The first break of the day is from ... to ... ."

Extra Road — Vers le Bac

5 **Search** the Internet and **find** what a morning school assembly is.

6 **Explain** in French the common points and the differences between this timetable and yours. Which timetable do you prefer? Why?

WHAT ABOUT YOU?

Which professional areas correspond to your job family?
aeronautics - beauty - business - catering - construction - engineering - graphics - hospitality - IT - logistics - maintenance - management - mechanics - transport - sales - sea - security - wood industry...

"It is never too late to be what you might have been."
George Eliot

TASK 3

OFFER HELP EE / Médiation Write a timetable and give information about it.
Your English-speaking classmate discovers his/her timetable but he/she doesn't understand it.
Write it in English and **explain** how it is organised.

Challenge yourself!

My Language Challenges	J'ai des difficultés ou je réponds non…
1. Je connais au moins 8 matières scolaires.	je fais le challenge n° 1.
2. Je suis capable de demander et dire l'heure, d'indiquer l'heure de début et de fin d'une activité. Je connais la différence entre *am* et *pm*.	je fais le challenge n° 2.
3. Je fais la différence entre la prononciation du « h » dans « *hour* » et dans « *half* ».	je fais le challenge n° 3.
4. Je sais comment est organisée la journée d'un élève britannique.	je fais le challenge n° 4.

Challenge 4

Challenge 1 WORDS AND CULTURE School Subjects

1 Take up the challenge!

Listez en anglais les différentes matières que vous avez pu avoir par le passé et les matières de votre emploi du temps actuel.

Mémorisez-les !

2 Find the word!

Fermez les yeux et **donnez** 8 matières scolaires.

Vérifiez vos réponses.

→ Method & Strategies
Tip 1 : Apprendre à mémoriser

Play with Words and Culture n° 5

Challenge 2 WORDS AND SENTENCES What time?

1 Take up the challenge!

Observez :

a. The school day starts at 08:30 am.
b. Lunch break is from 11:50 am to 12:30 pm.
c. The school day ends at 5:00 pm.

- À quoi correspondent les lettres *am* et *pm* ?
- **Associez** les horaires à leur lecture :
ten to twelve in the morning / half past eight in the morning / five o'clock in the afternoon / half past noon
- **Repérez** les prépositions qui précèdent les horaires. Qu'indiquent-elles ?

2 Find the rule!

- **Pour lire l'heure**, on indique :
  1. … .
  2. … dans la première demi-heure ou … dans la seconde demi-heure.
  3. … avant midi ou … après-midi.
- **Pour les heures piles**, on ajoute … derrière le nombre d'heures.
- « Et quart » et « moins le quart » se disent … et … .
- **Pour indiquer l'horaire** d'une activité (à …), on utilise la préposition … .
- **Pour indiquer les horaires de début et de fin** d'une activité, on utilise les prépositions … et … (de… à …).

RECAP > p. 124
Play with Words and Sentences n° 9 et 10

Challenge 3 WORDS AND SOUNDS The Sound /h/

1 Take up the challenge!

05 **Écoutez.**

a. and / hand b. eye / high c. art / heart
d. air / hair e. ear / hear

Quelle différence entendez-vous entre le premier et le second mot de chaque série ?

2 Find the sound!

La lettre … en début de mot doit, en général, être prononcée [h] : *hello* ; *hi* ; *happy* ; *how* ; *half*.

Elle peut permettre de faire la différence entre certains mots : *hand / and* ; *hair / air*.

Attention : dans quelques mots commençant par un « h », le son [h] ne s'entend pas : *hour*.

RECAP > p. 127
Play with Words and Sounds n° 12

Irregular Session

06 **Retrouvez** les trois verbes irréguliers ***learn***, ***teach*** et ***say*** dans le rabat à la fin du livre. **Écoutez**-les, **répétez**-les et **mémorisez**-les. **Révisez** les six verbes appris précédemment.

Play with...

WORDS AND CULTURE

1 **Spot** the odd one out!

a. The Indians – the Canadians – the French – the Australians

b. Irish – Spanish – English – Indian

c. Japanese – Canadian – Chinese – Portuguese

d. The Americans – the Britons – the South Africans – the Italians

2 **Find what languages these students speak.**

3 **RELAY RACE**

a. You've got 30 seconds to count as far as possible. Who is the strongest in your group?

b. Now count down from 100. Who is the winner now?

4 How do you say *59,390* in English?

5 a. **Match** the school subjects with the corresponding pictures.

Maths – Art & design – History – Geography – Foreign languages – Music – Science – PE or Physical Education (PE) – IT or Information Technology (IT) – Litterature

b. **Add** the professional subjects you learn and **find** a picture to illustrate them.

EXERCICES
Memory Game
Emotions
www.lienmini.fr/40241-06

WORDS AND SENTENCES

6 a. **Complete** Shakespeare's quote (from *Hamlet*) with the correct word.

"To ... or not to ... , that is the question."

b. **Complete** with the corresponding form of *be*.

1. I ... 17 years old.
2. My favourite school subject ... English.
3. ... you happy to be in a new class?
4. Next Saturday, my friends ... excited to come to my birthday party.
5. Where ... you born?
6. Last year, my sister ... at the university.

7 **Match** the question (a) and the answer (b).

a. How old is Pepper? / How are you? / How tall are you? / How far is your school from your house? / How does the interviewer feel?

b. He is confused. / It's 3 kms far from home. / I'm fine, thank you. / I'm 1.78 metres tall. / He's 4 years old.

8 **Choose** a sentence and write each word or group of words on a paper. Then put each in the right place. **Say** it out loud. Your partner may **correct** it if necessary. Then **switch** roles.

a. *there / English speakers / are / How many / in France?*

b. *in the class. / are / and 14 girls / 16 boys / There*

c. *There / in the class. / one English-speaker / is*

d. *robots / How many / are / in the world / there?*

e. *are / in the alphabet. / There / 26 letters*

9 **Write** the times of your timetable in full letters.

10 **DREAM TIMETABLE**

a. **Create** your ideal timetable. **Tell** your partner about it.

Example: On Monday, I have English from 8:05 (five past eight am) to 9:00 am (nine o'clock am).

b. **Listen to** your partner and **write** his/her ideal timetable.

c. **Compare** and **check**.

d. **Switch** roles.

WORDS AND SOUNDS

11 **Choose** a sentence from the list. **Say** it out loud! When your voice is rising, your classmates stand up. When it's falling, they sit down.

Tip: pay attention to *wh-* questions (↙) and *Yes-No* questions (↗).

a. How do you feel?
b. What is your favourite school subject?
c. Are you English?
d. How old are you?
e. What's your name?
f. Where do you live?
g. Do you speak German?
h. How many sisters have you got?
i. Have you got any brothers?
j. Is he your friend?

12 07 **TONGUE TWISTER**
Listen and **repeat**:

a. "*Irish wristwatch. Scottish witchcraft.*"

b. "*Helen's hamster hates ham.*"

MISSION CONTROL

Vers A2

SCENARIO You welcome a new English-speaking classmate. He/She doesn't speak French.

MISSION EOI / **Médiation** Ask and answer questions about your personal life and school days.

1. Par trois, **préparez** votre mission à l'aide des cartes suivantes et des expressions apprises dans l'unité.
2. **Prenez des notes** si besoin, mais ne les lisez pas lors de votre présentation. **Jouez** la scène !

STUDENT A

EOI

MISSION: Make your new English-speaking classmate feel welcome and ask him/her to introduce himself/herself. Answer his/her questions and help him/her to fit in well in the school and the class.

1. Welcome your English-speaking classmate.
3. Introduce yourself and get information about your classmate (name, age, date of birth, origins...).
5. Ask your classmate simple questions about the languages he/she can speak and the number of English speakers in his/her town.
7. Ask about the way your partner feels for his/her first day at school.
9. Offer assistance.
11. Give information about the school subjects and the starting and finishing times of the lessons.

KEY QUESTION Is meeting a foreign person an enriching or a disturbing experience? What do you think now?

STUDENT B

EOI

MISSION: You are an English-speaking student and it is your first day at school. One of your classmates welcomes you and asks questions to know you better. Answer and get information about your timetable.

2. Greet your classmate.
4. Introduce yourself and give personal information (name, age, date of birth, origins...).
6. Answer questions about the languages you can speak and the number of English-speakers in your town.
8. Tell about the way you feel.
10. Ask for help to understand your timetable.
12. Thank your classmate and ask other questions if needed.

STUDENT C

Médiation

MISSION: You listen to your partners and introduce your new English-speaking classmate to your class.

1. Listen to your partners and take notes about your English-speaking classmate.
2. Forward the information to introduce your English-speaking classmate to your class: name, age, origins, spoken languages, feelings, other English speakers in his/her town.
3. Ask your class to welcome your new friend.

Assess Yourself

Compétences de communication

- Comprendre et utiliser les formules de politesse et de prise de contact.
- Saluer et répondre aux questions me concernant (donner mon nom, mon âge, ma nationalité ; indiquer où j'habite ; dire comment je me sens).
- Poser des questions simples à un camarade et comprendre ses réponses.

Compétences linguistiques

- Utiliser le lexique approprié : formules de politesse, nombres, pays, nationalités, âge, emploi du temps... et le prononcer correctement.
- Conjuger correctement le verbe *être*.

Compétences transversales

- Comprendre et respecter la consigne.
- Collaborer et coopérer : partager une information ; accepter d'autres idées.

Micro Project

• Interdisciplinarité : éducation morale et civique – parcours citoyen

INTERCULTURAL WORLD PROJECT

You prepare an exhibition to show how intercultural your school and our world are!

1 Intercultural Schools...

Your school is an intercultural world.

➤ Where do your schoolmates come from?

1. **Interview** your schoolmates to learn where they come from.
2. **Prepare** a map to **tell** about their origins. **Look for** some information about the countries they come from (spoken languages, capital city, flag, number of inhabitants...) and **create** a poster about these countries.
3. **Read the text** and **explain** in French what an intercultural city is. **Make** a mindmap to show the themes your school may develop to become an intercultural school.

2 ... in an Intercultural World

We live in an intercultural world.

➤ Where do French-speaking people live?

1. **Search** the Internet.
2. **Prepare** a slideshow to say where French speaking people live in the world. Use a map to illustrate your answer.

3 Common Part

➤ Is diversity a strength at school? In the world? Why?

Use the documents you have created to **prepare** an exhibition for your class or your school to show how intercultural your school is in an intercultural world. You can use information you have learned about English-speaking persons in France as well.

What Is an Intercultural City?

Intercultural cities have a diverse population including people of different nationalities and origins, and with different languages or religions/beliefs. Most citizens regard diversity as a resource rather than a problem and accept that all cultures change as they encounter each other in the public arena. Intercultural city officials publicly advocate respect for diversity and a pluralistic city identity.

Some themes developed by intercultural cities : anti-rumours!; business and diversity; cultural heritage and diversity; gentrification, media and diversity.

Adapted from www.coe.int

Accompagner • Personnaliser

Apprendre à enrichir mon lexique

1. Prendre conscience de mes acquis

1 **Notez** toutes les langues que vous avez l'occasion d'entendre, de parler, de lire... dans votre famille, au cinéma, dans les jeux vidéo, sur des objets publicitaires, sur des livres et BD, dans le domaine culinaire...

2 **Notez** tous les mots anglais que vous trouvez autour de vous : dans la rue, sur les panneaux publicitaires, dans les titres de films, les noms de jeux vidéo, au restaurant, en sport... *English is easy and everywhere!*

2. Repérer les proximités lexicales entre le français et l'anglais

1 **Lisez** cet extrait de pièce de théâtre.

a. **Repérez** les mots transparents. En connaissez-vous d'autres ?

b. **Repérez** les mots empruntés à l'anglais dans ce texte français. Que remarquez-vous ? Connaissez-vous d'autres mots anglais utilisés dans la vie quotidienne ? **Classez**-les par catégorie (cinéma, nourriture, informatique, etc.).

c. **Cherchez** dans un dictionnaire bilingue la traduction des deux mots soulignés. Le sens des mots est-il identique en français et en anglais ? Qu'en est-il du mot « *chips* » ? Qu'en déduisez-vous ?

2 08 **Écoutez** ces phrases en anglais. Repérez les mots empruntés au français. Que remarquez-vous ?

Tea anyone ?
Ou vous préférez du vin ?
C'est rigolo n'est-ce pas ?
Le mot « culture » existe en anglais et en français
Culture : culture
Mais il ne nous rassemble pas au contraire il sert à distinguer nos mœurs
À dire que d'un côté de la Manche on fait comme ceci
Et que de l'autre on fait comme cela
En fait le français et l'anglais ont beaucoup de mots en commun
Nous partageons autant de mots que nous partageons d'histoire
À force de s'envahir tout de même on a fini par se mélanger
C'est amusant : Amusing
Intéressant : Interesting
Simple : Simple
Complicated : Compliqué
[...] Voilà tiens voilà le storyboard
« Il fait du foot, elle met des baskets, ils partent en voyage low-cost voir la jet-set du weekend, faut checker ça, lire le flyer, prendre un drink dans un after, ne pas être un has-been mais faire un best-of, porter un T-shirt oh so vintage et jouer dans un sitcom, c'est du fair-play, pas du bluff hein [...] »

I Kiss You ou l'hétéroglossie du bilinguisme, Catriona Morrison, Éditions Rhubarbe

3. Comprendre et construire des mots avec préfixes et suffixes

1 **Retrouvez** les radicaux de ces mots, le sens des préfixes et suffixes utilisés. Traduisez-les.

Exemples : unhappy = un/happy - happiness = happy/ness

childhood - dishonest - employee - employer - friendship - illegal - impossible - irregular - reunite - unemployment - valuable

2 **Ajoutez** des suffixes ou des préfixes et **construisez** des familles de mots à partir des noms suivants.

music - to train - comfort - easy - responsible

4. Repérer et comprendre des synonymes et des contraires

Associez les mots suivants (a) avec leurs synonymes (b) et/ou leurs antonymes (c).

a. good - happy - pretty - scared

b. attractive - delighted - frightened

c. angry - bad - ugly - sad

Accompagner ● Ouvrir, Orienter, Oser

Oser les langues dans ma vie personnelle, sociale et professionnelle

1. Comprendre l'importance de parler une langue étrangère

Lisez le texte et **expliquez** en quoi apprendre l'anglais est utile et important.

5 Advantages of English Language

1. One of the most dominating languages: it is an official language in 53 countries around the world and the second most common language in the world.
2. More career opportunities: used in international business, it will help you achieve all the goals of your career.
3. The top language of the Internet: English is one of the most used words on the Internet.
4. Make it easy to understand other languages: English is the most accessible language to learn, and it also makes it easier to understand other languages. It is a Germanic language. It uses many words from Romance languages as well (French, Spanish and Portuguese).
5. Access to a world of entertainment: many of the world's top films, books, and music are published and produced in English. Consequently, English gives access to a wealth of entertainment and enables you to understand the culture.

Adapted from https://neconnected.co.uk/

TIP
to achieve goals: atteindre des objectifs

2. Connaitre mes points d'appui en langue vivante et les leviers pour progresser

1 (09) **Écoutez** ces témoignages et **indiquez** :
a. L'origine de chaque locuteur. b. Le métier qu'il/elle envisage.

2 **Précisez** s'il/elle aime parler les langues vivantes étrangères et les raisons pour lesquelles il/elle souhaite ou a besoin de parler d'autres langues.

3 **Associez** chaque témoignage aux difficultés ainsi qu'aux points d'appui ou aux attitudes à développer pour progresser en langue.

Interlocuteurs : Arun / Jenna / Malo / Mia / Tim

Pays : Australia / France / India / New Zealand / Scotland

Métiers envisagés : a lorry-driver / a maintenance agent / a sales assistant / a waiter / a wedding planner

Raisons pour apprendre les langues : learning new facts / playing online with friends from all over the world / reading technical documents / speaking with customers / talking with people from other countries / travelling / watching films or series in English / working with English-speaking people

Points d'appui : can imitate sounds easily / have a good memory for new words / really motivated / don't mind making mistakes. What is important is to try! / try to improve myself! / really interested in talking with people from other countries / listen carefully / watch a lot of films or series in English / enjoy discovering new sounds / curious

Difficultés : have a bad pronunciation / It's difficult to remember words / find it difficult to take risks! / not very good at understanding when people speak

3. Oser

Appuyez-vous sur les témoignages entendus pour exprimer vos gouts et donner votre opinion sur vos propres compétences en langues vivantes (difficultés, points d'appui). **Utilisez** des expressions de gout, d'opinion, ainsi que l'expression de la cause (*because, as*).

→ **FLAP:** Likes and Dislikes, Opinions

UNIT 2 Footsteps

Vers A2 +

- Habitudes et modes de vie
- Professionnels célèbres

Look at the document and **describe** what you see.
What is a role model for you?

YOUR ROAD MAP

www.lienmini.fr/40241-07

UP TO YOU!

- Easy Road
- Extra Road
- Bonus Road

KEY QUESTION How important is it for young people to have a role model?

SCENARIO Your school organises a career exploration fair.

TASK 1 A FAST AND FURIOUS SCHEDULE EOC Present a typical day in the life of a successful person.

TASK 2 INSPIRING PEOPLE EE Pay tribute to someone you admire.

MISSION EE Write an article for the event leaflet to present the daily life of a successful person you admire (businessman/woman, athlete, chef, artist...) and explain why he/she is a strong role model for you.

to Success

Open up!

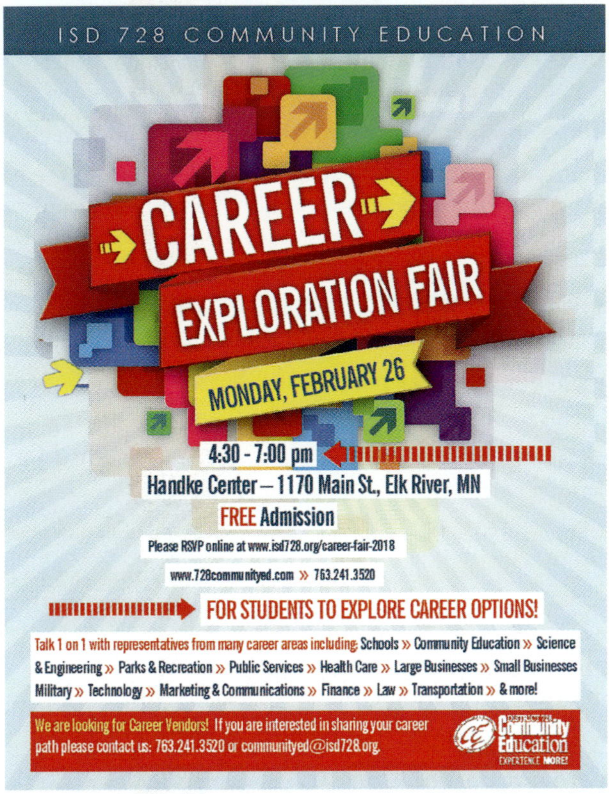

Look at the picture.

1. What type of document is it?
2. What event is promoted? **Explain** what it consists in.
3. **Make** sentences to give as many details as possible about this fair (date, place, time, admission fees, contacts you can make...).

WHAT ABOUT YOU?

1. What job do you want to do in the future?
2. Do you think it's important to talk to skilled professionals before choosing a career? Why?

Get ready!

In-Class Activities

EXERCICES
Flashcards
www.lienmini.fr/40241-08

1. **Look at** the flashcards and **listen** to the words. **Repeat.**
2. **Memorise** the way the words are written.
3. **Mime** a daily activity to your classmates. Then **switch** roles.

By yourself!

1. 10 **Listen** and **memorise.**
2. **Use** the words you have just learned to **fill in** the gaps.
   a. If you like preparing food, you could be a ... .
   b. If you like serving customers at their tables, you could be a ... .
   c. If you like creating clothes, you could be a ... .
   d. If you like playing sports, you could be a ... .
   e. If you like preparing bread and cakes, you could be a ... .
   f. If you like travelling by plane, you could be a ... .
   g. If you like greeting and dealing with visitors, you could be a ... .

A Crazy Schedule!

Elon Musk's Daily Routine Will Blow Your Mind

The daily routine of a genius like Elon Musk, the CEO of Tesla and SpaceX, isn't an easy one. So what's a day in the life of Elon Musk like?

Start early! By 7 am, Elon Musk is already up and working out how to make the most of the day*.

Breakfast? I'm good, thanks! He doesn't really have breakfast, but might occasionally grab a cup of coffee and an omelet.

Jump in the shower: Showering is one habit Elon Musk never breaks.

The five-minute meeting: As soon as Elon Musk leaves the house he's got people waiting for him with meetings and engagements. To manage things, and ensure he sees to everything and everyone, he schedules all his appointments* in five-minute blocks. His typical working week adds up 85-100 hours.

Tesla, his most demanding baby: Elon dedicates Tuesdays, Wednesdays, and Thursdays to his auto company, which adds up to 42 hours a week devoted to Tesla. SpaceX, which aims to populate Mars and conquer the Moon, gets Mondays and Fridays.

No e-mail, no phone calls: He doesn't spend much time answering phone calls and e-mails.

Lights out! Elon won't go to bed until he's made sure to deal with all his to-do's. He slides into bed around 1 am.

There's even time for hobbies: In a packed life, Elon somehow still finds time to pursue his passions. Reading is one of them, and he spends a couple of minutes a day on it. He also goes to the gym at least twice a week.

Adapted from https://us.hola.com

TIPS

appointment: un rendez-vous
make the most of: tirer le meilleur parti de

1 **Read** the title and the introduction. Then **look at** the picture. What and who is the text about? **Give** as much information as you can about that man (job, nationality, reasons for his fame...).

2 **Read** the text carefully and **select** the activities which are not part of Elon Musk's daily routine.
wake up early - play video games - work out - have a shower - answer phone calls and e-mails - attend appointments - take a nap - update his blog - read

3 **Form** groups of 3 to **answer** the following questions in less than 5 minutes.
a. What does Elon Musk occasionally have for breakfast?
b. How many hours a week does he work?
c. What time does he go to bed every night?
d. How does he share his time between Tesla and SpaceX?

→ Method & Strategies
Tip 3 : Comprendre un support écrit

Extra Road — Vers le Bac

4 **Read** the text again and **answer** the following questions.
a. What is the necessary condition for Elon Musk to go to bed?
b. How long do his appointments last?
c. What does Tesla company manufacture?
d. What is SpaceX's long term goal?

WHAT ABOUT YOU?

Could you run your day as Elon Musk runs his? Why? Why not?

“I never dreamed about success, I worked for it.”
Estée Lauder

TASK 1

A FAST AND FURIOUS SCHEDULE EOC **Present a typical day in the life of a successful person:** Dwayne Johnson, the American-Canadian actor, producer, businessman and retired professional wrestler (See Annex p.112).

Challenge yourself!

My Language Challenges	J'ai des difficultés ou je réponds non...
1. Je connais des adverbes et des marqueurs de fréquence et je sais où les placer dans la phrase.	je fais le challenge n° 1.
2. Je suis capable d'utiliser le présent simple (formes affirmative et négative).	je fais le challenge n° 2.
3. Je sais prononcer correctement le « -s » à la 3e personne du singulier au présent simple.	je fais le challenge n° 3.
4. Je connais au moins 6 expressions idiomatiques.	je fais le challenge n° 4.

Challenge 4

Challenge 1 WORDS AND CULTURE Frequency

1 Take up the challenge!

Observez :

a. He never stops working.

b. Everyday, he gets up at 7 am.

c. He goes to the gym twice a week.

Repérez les adverbes ou indicateurs de fréquence. En connaissez-vous d'autres ?

2 Find the word!

- **Les adverbes de fréquence** se placent toujours ... le verbe, sauf lorsqu'il s'agit de *be*.
- **Les indicateurs de fréquence :** *Every* + nom singulier (*weekend*, ..., ..., ...) et ... (1x) *a day, twice* (2x) *a week*, ... (3x) *a month* se placent ... ou ... de phrase.

Play with Words and Culture n° 1 et 2

Challenge 2 WORDS AND SENTENCES Daily Routine

1 Take up the challenge!

Observez :

a. Elon sleeps for just six hours.

b. He doesn't really have breakfast.

c. He goes to bed around 1 am.

d. I admire him.

Repérez les groupes verbaux.

- Quel temps est employé ? Que permet-il d'exprimer ?
- Comment le conjugue-t-on à la forme affirmative ? négative ?

2 Find the rule!

Le ... permet d'exprimer ... .

- **à la forme affirmative :** *I / You / We / They* + ... *He / She / It* + ... **ou** ... pour les verbes qui se terminent par « s », « z », « x », « sh », « ch » et « o ».
- **à la forme négative :** *I / You / We / They* + ... + BV **ou** *He / She / It* + ... + BV.

RECAP > p. 124
Play with Words and Sentences n° 7 et 8

Challenge 3 WORDS AND SOUNDS The Letter "s" at the End of a Verb

1 Take up the challenge!

11 **Écoutez et soyez attentif à la prononciation du « -s » à la fin des verbes.**

a. Elon Musk dedicates Tuesdays to Tesla, his auto company.

b. At the weekend, he chooses to stay home. He finds time to pursue his passion.

Que remarquez-vous ?

2 Find the sound!

Le « -s » qui marque la 3e personne du singulier au présent simple se prononce :

- ... **après une consonne « sourde »** (p, t, k et f) : *he stops / he eats*.
- ... **après une voyelle** ou **une consonne « sonore »** (b, d, g, m, l, n, v, etc.) : *he goes / he finds*.
- ... **après un son « sifflant »** (/dʒ/, /s/, /z/, /ʃ/, /tʃ/) : *he kisses / he buzzes*.

RECAP > p. 127
Play with Words and Sounds n° 11

Irregular Session

12 **Retrouvez** les trois verbes irréguliers *spend*, *read* et *wake up* dans le rabat à la fin du livre. **Écoutez**-les, **répétez**-les et **mémorisez**-les.

Iconic Role Models

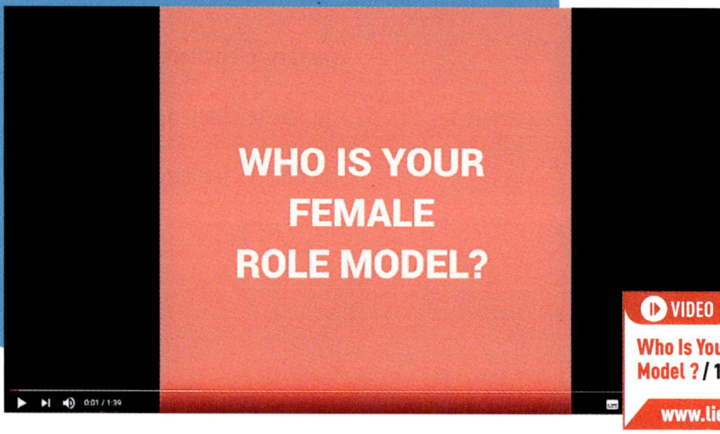

VIDEO
Who Is Your Role Model ? / 1'39
www.lienmini.fr/40241-09

→ Method & Strategies
Tip 3 : Comprendre un support audio ou vidéo

1 **Watch** the video. What type of video is it? Who can you see? What are these people doing?

2 **Watch** again. Try to find who's who!

- a. A Nobel Peace Prize recipient defending education rights.
- b. A gorgeous actress involved in the HeForShe campaign.
- c. The first female justice to serve on the Supreme Court.
- d. An incredibly beautiful model breaking barriers and stereotypes.

1. Emma Watson
2. Malala Yousafzai
3. Ashley Graham
4. Sandra Day O'Connor

3 **Last viewing. Explain** why these celebrities are role models for teenage girls.

Lady Gaga

Ellen Degeneres

Amal Clooney

WHAT ABOUT YOU?

According to you, which qualities are essential to be a good role model?

Extra Road Vers le Bac

4 **Focus** on the last two candidates and answer these questions.
a. Who is Kelsey's role model? What happened to this person and what has she learned from her?
b. Why is Jaanu inspired by her grandmother?

“I don't want to be a supermodel; I want to be a role model.”
Queen Latifah

TASK 2

INSPIRING PEOPLE EE Pay tribute to someone you admire.

1 **Think about** a person close to you who influences you in a positive way, someone who motivates you to do great things (family member, sports coach, teacher, friend...).

2 **Write** him/her a thank you message explaining what you admire about him/her.

Challenge yourself!

My Language Challenges	J'ai des difficultés ou je réponds non...
1. Je connais au moins 6 adjectifs pour qualifier une personne que j'admire.	je fais le challenge n° 1.
2. Je maitrise la place et l'ordre des adjectifs.	je fais le challenge n° 2.
3. Je sais reconnaitre et prononcer un adjectif composé.	je fais le challenge n° 3.
4. Je connais l'objectif du mouvement HeforShe.	je fais le challenge n° 4.

Challenge 4

Challenge 1 WORDS AND CULTURE Qualities of a Role Model

1 Take up the challenge!

Retrouvez dans la liste suivante les qualités évoquées dans la vidéo et identifiez les défauts qui s'y sont glissés.

beautiful - brave - cheerful - clever - committed - courageous - elegant - energetic - fabulous - generous - gorgeous - humble - lazy - mean - motivated - outspoken - plain - reliable - selfish - smart - talented - tolerant - world-renowned

2 Find the word!

- **Retrouvez** les adjectifs qui correspondent aux définitions suivantes. **Proposez** un équivalent français pour chacun d'entre eux.
particularly happy and optimistic - devoted to a cause or a person - very active - speaking in an honest and open way - capable of being trusted - intelligent
- 13 **Écoutez, répétez et mémorisez** les 6 adjectifs trouvés. Puis **listez-les** à votre voisin(e) sans aucune aide.

Play with Words and Culture n° 3, 4, 5 et 6

Challenge 2 WORDS AND SENTENCES Adjectives: Position in Sentences

1 Take up the challenge!

Observez :

a. Zendaya is a fabulous 23-year-old American actress.
b. Malala Yousafzai is brave and intelligent.

Repérez les adjectifs.

- À quoi servent-ils ?
- Où sont-ils placés par rapport aux noms qu'ils qualifient ?

2 Find the rule!

- **Les adjectifs épithètes** se placent ... le nom qu'ils qualifient. Quand il y a plusieurs adjectifs devant un nom, ils sont placés du plus subjectif au plus objectif : jugement personnel, puis information sur la taille, l'âge, la couleur, l'origine, la matière.
- **Les adjectifs attributs** se placent ... un verbe d'état (*be, seem, look...*).

RECAP > p. 124
Play with Words and Sentences n° 9 et 10

Challenge 3 WORDS AND SOUNDS Compound Adjectives

1 Take up the challenge!

14 **Écoutez, repérez les adjectifs et soyez attentif à leur terminaison.**

a. Ashley Graham is a super-talented model.
b. Amal Clooney is a world-renowned attorney.
c. Emma Watson is a nice-looking girl.

2 Find the sound!

Les adjectifs composés se forment de plusieurs façons :

- adverbe + adj. en *-ed* : *super-talented* ;
- nom + adjectif en *-ed* : *world-renowned* ;
- adj. + nom complété par *-ed* : *blue-eyed* ;
- adj. + BV en *-ing* : *nice-looking*.

Soyez attentif à la prononciation des terminaisons de ces adjectifs !

Play with Words and Sounds n° 12

Irregular Session

15 **Retrouvez** les trois verbes irréguliers ***feel***, ***be*** et ***show*** dans le rabat à la fin du livre. **Écoutez**-les, **répétez**-les et **mémorisez**-les. **Révisez** les trois verbes appris précédemment.

Play with...

WORDS AND CULTURE

1 **Use** the anagrams and **find** the adverbs corresponding to the right lines.

LAERYR

NOTEF

WYASLA

LAUSYUL

MIMOSTESE

RYDAHL VERE

VERNE

2 **Rewrite** the sentences putting the elements in brackets at the right place.

a. The students are late. (never)

b. She eats meat. (hardly ever)

c. You go to bed at midnight. (sometimes)

d. I am tired after my school day. (often)

e. I eat at the canteen. (twice a week)

f. He plays baseball. (every week)

3 **Complete** the sentences with the right adjectives.

elegant - reliable - clever - outspoken - cheerful - energetic

a. My friend Amy is very ... . She is good at learning things.

b. How can you be so ... at 6 am?

c. He is very ... . He always says what he thinks.

d. Michelle Obama is an ... lady who is always beautifully dressed.

e. We need a young and ... candidate for this position.

f. My dad is a very ... person. If he says he'll do something, he'll do it!

4 **BOARD RACE "QUALITIES"!**

5 min

a. **Build up** a team. Each team **lines up** in front of the board. Students at the front **get** a marker.

b. When your teacher says "Go!", you have to race to **write** a personal quality on the board. Then, **pass** the marker to the next student and **go** to the **back** of the line.

The winning team is the one who correctly writes the largest number of adjectives in 5 minutes.

*NB: you can **correct** one of your teammates' proposal. In this case, you can't propose a new adjective.*

5 **Choose** an inspirational woman or man from the present day or the past. **Write** an acrostic poem about her/him using the letters of her/his name and adjectives.

Beyoncé
B *is for beautiful*
E *is for enthusiastic*
Y *is for young*
O *is for obstinate*
N *is for nice*
C *is for clever*
E *is for elegant*

6 **Change** negative adjectives into positive ones to **correct** this presentation about the singer of The Weeknd.

a. The Weeknd is a talentless and unknown Canadian R&B singer.

b. He is a very inactive artist and writes his own songs and lyrics.

c. He collaborates with many stars and likes sharing his talent: he is such a selfish person!

d. Drake or Sia, who often work with him, think he is a mean guy and has a horrible voice.

WORDS AND SENTENCES

7 **Use** the verbs in brackets to **complete** the sentences about Zuckerberg's daily routine.

a. Zuckerberg ... (take) his time getting up in the morning and ... (not get out) of bed before 8 am.

b. The first thing he ... (do) when he ... (wake up) is check Facebook, Messenger and WhatsApp.

c. He ... (like) keeping his body healthy, so he ... (hit) the gym every morning.

d. Actually, he ... (go) for a morning run with his dog Beast, his favourite running partner.

e. Although Zuckerberg ... (spend) more hours in the office than the average employee, he still ... (find) time to pay attention to the things he ... (love) to do.

f. His wife, Priscilla Chan, is Chinese, and he ... (try) to learn Mandarin when he ... (have) a free moment.

Adapted from https://www.cheatsheet.com

8 **Use** the simple present and **complete** with the negative form when needed.

a. I ... (admire) Peter Diamandis, the brilliant entrepreneur. Like him, I ... (want) to earn money for myself but I ... (want) to have money to address the biggest challenges we ... (face) today.

b. My friends ... (have) another role model, Richard Branson. They ... (envy) his fortune but they ... (appreciate) his attitude. He ... (be) so joyful.

9 **Reorder** these elements to form correct sentences.

a. *beautiful / three / they / young / children / have / .*

b. *is / handsome / boy / a / Chris / dark-haired / .*

c. *tonight / absolutely / gorgeous / look / you / !*

d. *Italian / a / he / flashy / drives / car / .*

e. *hair / deep / wavy / she / eyes / is / a / blue / girl / with / long / lovely / and / blond / .*

10 **Put** the adjectives in the right order to qualify the nouns.

a. A singer → young / English / talented

b. A scarf → blue / stylish / woolen

c. A post-box → red / lovely / old

WORDS AND SOUNDS

11 a. How do you **pronounce** the final "s"? **Associate** these verbs with the right sound.

relaxes - dances - writes - travels - leaves - cooks - washes - sleeps - sings

"/s/"

"/z/"

"/iz/"

b. 16 **Listen to** the recording and **correct** your mistakes if necessary.

12 a. **Form** compound adjectives using one word of each list.

Student A	Student B
easy	*eyed*
well	*headed*
world	*going*
home	*natured*
hard	*famous*
green	*dressed*
good	*made*
big	*working*

b. **Choose** 3 compound adjectives you found and **say** them out loud. Let your partner **check** your pronunciation.

MISSION CONTROL

Vers A2 +

SCENARIO Your school organises a career exploration fair.

MISSION EE Write an article for the event leaflet to present the daily life of a successful person you admire (businessman/woman, athlete, chef, artist...) and explain why he/she is a strong role model for you.

→ Method & Strategies
Tip 5 : S'exprimer à l'écrit

1. **Choisissez** une personne dont la carrière est un modèle pour vous (homme ou femme d'affaires, athlète, artiste, chef...).
2. **Utilisez** la carte suivante pour organiser votre portrait et expliquez pourquoi vous admirez cette personne. Vous pouvez également ajouter d'autres informations.
3. **Écrivez** votre article. Utilisez le présent simple pour parler des habitudes de vie. N'oubliez pas d'ajouter des adverbes de fréquence.
4. **Relisez** attentivement votre premier écrit et complétez-le avec des mots de liaisons (voir rabats).
5. **Finalisez** votre article. **Choisissez** un titre et **ajoutez** une photo.

The Crazy Schedule of my Role Model

Name: ____________________

Date and place of birth: ____________________

Age: ____________________

Nationality: ____________________

Job: ____________________

Daily routine: ____________________

Qualities I admire: ____________________

Special features: ____________________

KEY QUESTION How important is it for young people to have a role model? What do you think now?

Assess Yourself

Compétences de communication

- Comprendre et présenter la vie quotidienne d'une personne.
- Parler de ses qualités humaines et professionnelles.
- Exprimer la fréquence d'une activité.

Compétences linguistiques

- Utiliser le lexique approprié : activités du quotidien et métiers.
- Placer correctement les adjectifs par rapport aux noms qu'ils qualifient.
- Utiliser le présent simple.

Compétences transversales

- Comprendre et respecter la consigne.
- Organiser mon écrit de façon cohérente.
- Présenter correctement mon article.

Exam Road

COMPRÉHENSION DE L'ÉCRIT

CO
EOC-EOI

25 Entrepreneurs on the Celebrities Who Inspire Them

February 24, 2020

Inspiration can come from anywhere – sometimes from people. Celebrities are often seen as the epitome* of success and inspiration. For some entrepreneurs, that can be a major motivating factor. [...]

"Alicia Keys is an inspiring celebrity because she is not only a wonderful role model to young women and a fabulous singer and pianist, but she also embraces the art of giving back to humanity through her philanthropic efforts. Through her nonprofit Keep a Child Alive foundation, she provides medicine to Africans living with HIV and AIDS. Her donations to the youth also provides scholarships* to children in need. Alicia Keys has also used her music in times of destruction during Hurricane Katrina, Hurricane Sandy and the earthquake in Haiti. I admire what she does nationally and internationally. It's always nice to see artists give back, and she seems to do it with so much humility and grace." – Erik Humphrey, publisher and CEO of Quiet on the Set Magazine.

www.businessnewsdaily.com

TIPS

epitome: un modèle
scholarship: une bourse

Lisez le texte ci-dessus puis **répondez** en français aux questions.

1. De quel type de document s'agit-il ?
2. Que représentent souvent les célébrités pour les entrepreneurs ?
3. Citez les différentes raisons pour lesquelles A. Keys est une source d'inspiration pour E. Humphrey.
4. Précisez deux actions menées par la fondation d'A. Keys « Keep a child alive ».
5. A. Keys s'est aussi mobilisée pour aider les populations après des catastrophes naturelles. Lesquelles ?
6. Quelles sont les qualités personnelles qu'E. Humphrey admire le plus chez A. Keys ?

→ **Vers le Bac** À partir de vos éléments de réponse, rédigez un compte-rendu en français du support. Vous préciserez la nature et le thème principal, les informations importantes ainsi que la fonction du document.

EXPRESSION ÉCRITE

Vous **traiterez**, en anglais et en 80 mots minimum, le sujet suivant.

Rappel : l'attendu au baccalauréat sera de 100 à 120 mots.

Sujet :

Do you need to be passionate about your job to live a fulfilling life? Justify your answer.

Accompagner • Personnaliser

Apprendre à mémoriser

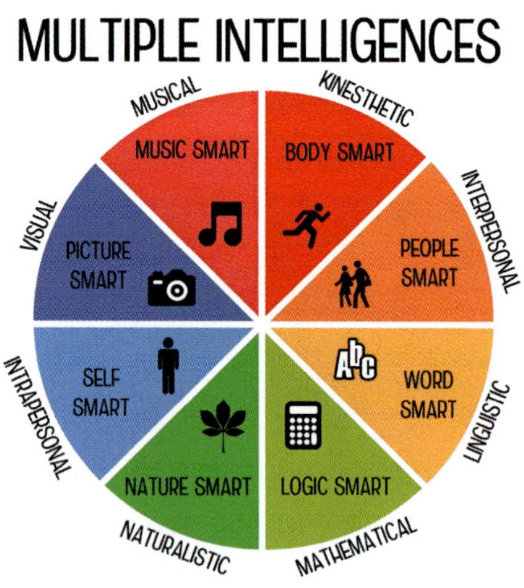

1. Identifier mes intelligences

Faites le test des intelligences multiples dans votre Bonus Road et **découvrez** comment vous **mémorisez**.

➔ **Method & Strategies**
Tip 1 : Apprendre à mémoriser

2. Jouer avec mes intelligences

EXERCICES
Flashcards
www.lienmini.fr/40241-10

1 **Réalisez** les activités suivantes et **déterminez** les intelligences sollicitées.

Activité 1 : At school

a. **Regardez** les flashcards, **cliquez** et **écoutez**. **Imitez**, **répétez** à voix basse puis à voix haute.

b. **Retrouvez** les mots à partir des illustrations. **Enregistrez**-vous, puis **corrigez**-vous.

c. CHAIN CONVERSATION **Complétez** la phrase suivante en ajoutant un des mots mémorisés : *« In my schoolbag, there is... »* Votre voisin répète et ajoute un autre mot...

d. CHINESE WHISPER **Choisissez** un mot de la liste, **transmettez**-le à voix basse à votre voisin, qui le transmet à son tour. Le dernier du groupe répète à voix haute. **Corrigez** !

Activité 2 : At work

a. **Regardez** les flashcards. **Photographiez** l'image et **écoutez**. **Répétez** et **corrigez** entre pairs.

b. KIM'S GAME Une flashcard a disparu. Laquelle ?

Activité 3 : Mix it up!

a. **Cliquez** à nouveau sur les flashcards des activités 1 et 2 et **observez** l'écriture des mots. **Lisez** à voix haute ou à voix basse, **épelez** ou **recopiez** les mots.

b. **Regardez** les images et **complétez** avec les lettres manquantes :

1. a s_ _ _ _ _b_g / a r_ _ _r / a p_ _ _ _l / a h_ _ _l_ _ _ _ _r / a p_n / s_ _ _ _ _ _s / a r_ _ _ _r / a p_ _ _r-c_ _p
2. *a t_ _l / a f_ _ _r / a s_ _ _ _ _ _n / a s_ _ _ _ _ _ _ _ _r / a p_ _e / a s_ _ _ _h / a f_ _ _ _r / a k_ _ _ _ _ _d / a p_ _ _ _ _r*

2 Selon votre profil, **construisez** une activité pour mémoriser à l'oral, puis à l'écrit :

a. le plus de mots possibles dans la liste suivante :

kind, lazy, ungrateful, impatient, caring, violent, rude, hard-working, intolerant, reliable, honest, unreliable, dishonest, sensitive, patient, aggressive, thoughtful, motivated, revengeful, indecisive, moody, stubborn, selfish

b. les phrases suivantes, puis le texte complet :

a. ***Kim Kardashian is an American model, a businesswoman and an actress.***

b. ***She has meetings every day.***

3. Associer mes intelligences et mes compétences

VIDEO
You Think You Are Smart? There Are 9 Types of Intelligence! / 4'56
www.lienmini.fr/40241-43

1 **Regardez** le début de la vidéo et **donnez** le maximum d'informations concernant le projet évoqué.

2 **Regardez** chacun deux extraits différents de la vidéo. **Échangez** pour **associer** les experts à leurs compétences, leur rôle dans le projet et l'intelligence qu'ils illustrent.

3 **Identifiez**-vous à l'un des experts et **justifiez** en anglais.

Tips
D'autres stratégies pour mémoriser des énoncés, des textes et votre leçon dans votre Bonus Road !

Accompagner • Consolider

Parler de moi, parler des autres

Irregular Fight

1. Odd one out

1 **Chassez** l'intrus dans chaque série.

a. waiter / attorney / cheerful / vet / chef
b. sometimes / gorgeous / always / usually
c. outspoken / never / reliable / smart
d. Australian / Canadian / Japanese / Italian
e. Irish / British / Belgian / English / Spanish
f. American / African / Scottish / German
g. Indian / French / Welsh / technology
h. business / catering / timetable / construction / social care

2 17 **Lisez** ces mots à voix haute à votre voisin, puis **vérifiez** la prononciation.

3 Pour chaque série, **imaginez** une phrase dans laquelle vous utiliserez un des mots proposés.

2. Daily Routine Activities

Rédigez des phrases à partir des pictogrammes suivants. **Retranscrivez** les horaires en toutes lettres.

a.				**She...**
b.				**I...**
c.				**He...**

3. Unscramble it!

1 **Lisez** les questions ci-dessous et **retrouvez** les réponses. Attention, les mots de ces réponses sont un peu emmêlés...

1. What's your name?
2. How are you?
3. What nationality are you?
4. How old are you?
5. Where are you from?
6. What is your main subject at school?
7. What are your main qualities?
8. Who is your role model?
9. What job do you want to do in the future?

a. electronics. / It is
b. cheerful. / am / and / I / generous
c. fine, / am / I / you. / thank
d. 'm / English. / I
e. because / talented, intelligent and hard-working. / is / Lewis Hamilton / he is / My role model
f. want / a car mechanic. / to be / I
g. am / 15 / I / old. / years
h. My / is / George. / name
i. from / 'm / I / London.

2 **Jouez** la conversation avec votre voisin.

UNIT 3 Faster,

Vers A2 +

- Grandes manifestations
- Sports nationaux et équipes célèbres

Look at the document and **describe** what you see.
Which sport are the young men playing? For which event?

YOUR ROAD MAP

www.lienmini.fr/40241-11

UP TO YOU!

- Easy Road
- Extra Road
- Bonus Road

KEY QUESTION **Do Olympic sports reflect national or international values?**

SCENARIO **The IOC (International Olympic Committee) is preparing the Olympic Games for 2032. It invites young people to create a video to highlight a new sport and include it to the programme of the Olympic Games.**

TASK 1 SURVEY SET **EE** Create a survey to identify your class's favourite sport.

TASK 2 PRESENTATION TIME **EE** / **EOC** Create the ID card of your favourite sport and present it to your classmates.

TASK 3 FINAL MATCH **EE** / **Médiation** Create a poster listing the six most important skills and values in sports and present it.

MISSION **EOC** **In a one-minute video, present the popular sport you would like to add to the Olympic Games.**

Higher, Stronger

Open up!

Rio2016

TOKYO 2020

Postponed to...

PARiS 2024

LA 28

1. **Look at** the pictures.
   a. What sort of documents are they?
   b. What is the common point?
   c. What do you notice about the dates?
2. What does "LA" stand for? In which continent is this city? What about the other cities? **Check** your answers with your partner.

WHAT ABOUT YOU?

1. Which is your favourite logo? **Explain** your choice to your group.
2. **Imagine** the logo for the following Olympic Games. **Draw** it and **describe** it to your partners.

Get ready!

In-Class Activities

EXERCICES
Flashcards
www.lienmini.fr/40241-12

1. **Look at** the flashcards and **listen** to the words. **Repeat.**
2. **Memorise** the way the words are written.
3. **Choose** a sport and **describe** it to your partner. He/she **writes** his/her answer. **Check** it then **swap** roles.

By yourself!

The Youth Olympic Games also include five *Learn & Share activities*, built around five key themes.

1. **Search** the Internet to find these themes and **look for** the translations.
2. **Memorise** these themes.

1. READING ROAD
Vers A2 +

No Pain, No Gain!

Student Athletic Interest Survey* – Northwest Career And Technical High School, Lakewood, WA, USA

This survey helps schools determine student interest in specific sports so they can plan which sports to offer to equally meet the interests of male and female students.

1. In the last school year, have you participated in sports at your school?
☐ Yes. Please list all of the sports you play at your school: ...
☒ No. If not, what were your reasons? Select all that apply.
☐ I'm not interested in playing any sport. ☒ The sport I like is not offered at my school.
☐ I'm too busy with school.

2. Do you currently play a sport outside of your school sports program?
☒ Yes. Please list all of the sports you play outside of your school sports program: → Basketball, Lacrosse
☐ No.

3. Does your school offer all the sports you are interested in playing? ☐ Yes ☒ No

4. Considering your time, interests and responsibilities, which of the following sports would you most like to participate in at your school? Select up to 3 sports.
☐ Badminton ☐ Baseball ☒ Basketball ☐ Bowling ☐ Cross country ☐ Field hockey ☐ Football ☒ Golf ☐ Gymnastics ☒ Lacrosse ☐ Rowing/Crew ☐ Soccer ☐ Softball ☐ Swimming and diving ☐ Tennis ☐ Track and field ☐ Ultimate frisbee ☐ Volleyball ☐ Water polo ☐ Weightlifting ☐ Wrestling ☐ Other.
☐ None. I don't plan to play sports at school.

Adapted from https://www.k12.wa.us

TIP
A survey is used to collect opinions.

1 Look at the title and the source of the document.
a. What type of document is it? What is it about?
b. Which country does it concern? Which state?

→ Method & Strategies
Tip 3 : Comprendre un support écrit

2 Read the questions in the document. Find a synonym for *attracted by* and for *choose*. **Give** an opposite of *inside*.

3 Have a look at Lucy's answers. **Choose** the correct sentences and **transform** the wrong ones.
a. She didn't participate in any sports in her school last year because she doesn't like sports.
b. She doesn't play sports outside of her school.
c. She wants to practise three sports at her school.

4 Have a look at the information below and **find** how many students have answered the survey.
a. In Lucy's class. b. In her school.

75% of Lucy's classmates have answered | 24 students in Lucy's class | ½ of the school's students have completed the survey | 244 students in the school

WHAT ABOUT YOU?

1 Ask the questions of the survey to your partner. **Take** notes.

2 Present his/her answers to the class. **Swap** roles.

Extra Road Vers le Bac

5 **Write** questions that could be added to the survey.

"Champions keep playing until they get it right."
Billie Jean King

TASK 1

SURVEY SET EE Create a survey to identify your class's favourite sport.
Ask questions about the sports your classmates practise or support.

Challenge yourself!

My Language Challenges	J'ai des difficultés ou je réponds non…
1. Je connais les verbes de gout, d'appréciation.	je fais le challenge n° 1.
2. Je sais poser des questions au présent simple.	je fais le challenge n° 2.
3. Je suis capable de présenter les résultats d'un sondage.	je fais le challenge n° 3.
4. Je distingue l'écriture de certains mots en anglais britannique et américain.	je fais le challenge n° 4.

Challenge 4

Challenge 1 WORDS AND CULTURE Likes and Dislikes

1 Take up the challenge!

Observez :

a. The sport I like is not offered at my school.

b. My brother dislikes baseball.

c. I am keen on practising soccer.

d. Do you enjoy playing cricket?

- **Qu'expriment les verbes ou expressions soulignés ?**
- **Connaissez-vous d'autres verbes ou expressions qui expriment cette notion ?**

2 Find the word!

To like, to enjoy, to be keen on sont des verbes ou expressions qui servent à exprimer … .

100% → 0%

- Be keen on
- enjoy
- like
- don't/doesn't mind
- dislike
- hate

→ **FLAP:** Likes and Dislikes

Play with Words and Culture n° 1

Challenge 2 WORDS AND SENTENCES Simple Present/Questions

1 Take up the challenge!

Observez :

a. Do you play a sport outside of your school sports programme? Yes, I do. / No, I don't.

b. Does your school offer all the sports you are interested in playing? Yes, it does. / No, it doesn't.

c. Which sports do you like? I love baseball and soccer.

- **Par quels mots commencent les deux premières phrases ?**
- **Repérez** les auxiliaires et les verbes : où se situent-ils ?
- Comment répond-on à chacune des questions ?

2 Find the rule!

- **Pour les questions fermées au présent simple** (réponse attendue : oui/non), on utilise l'auxiliaire … à toutes les personnes ou … à la 3ᵉ personne du singulier. L'auxiliaire est suivi du sujet et de la … .
- **Pour les questions ouvertes au présent simple** (réponse attendue : une information), on ajoute un mot interrogatif en début de question.

→ **FLAP:** Questions Words

RECAP > p. 125
Play with Words and Sentences n° 5

Challenge 3 WORDS AND SOUNDS Percentage and Fraction

1 Take up the challenge!

18 **Écoutez** et **soyez attentif** à la prononciation des pourcentages et des fractions.

a. 75% of her classmates have answered the survey.

b. In her high school, ½ of the students have completed the survey.

Transformez les pourcentages en fractions et inversement.

2 Find the sound!

- Pour parler des résultats d'un sondage, on utilise des pourcentages : 75 … = 75 per cent.
- Ces résultats peuvent être traduits sous la forme de fractions.
- a half = … ; a quarter = … ; one third = … ; two-fifths = … .

Attention : half : /ˈhæf/ ; quarter : /ˈkwɔrtɚ/ ; fifth : /ˈfɪfθ/.

→ **FLAP:** Numbers

Play with Words and Sounds n° 10

Irregular Session

19 **Retrouvez** les trois verbes irréguliers *see*, *keep* et *hit* dans le rabat à la fin du livre. **Écoutez**-les, **répétez**-les et **mémorisez**-les.

Game, Set and Match

VIDEO
One Minute, One Sport : Softball / 1'19
www.lienmini.fr/40241-13

→ Method & Strategies
Tip 3 : Comprendre un support écrit

1. **Watch** the video. **Pay attention** to the pictures and **answer** the questions.
   a. How many sports are there in the Tokyo Summer Olympics?
   b. Which sport is the video about?
   c. Which sport is it compared to?

2. **Read** the subtitles of the video. **Pay attention to** the key words and **find** the key information about this sport in each part of the video.
   a. Part 1 of the video (from the beginning to 0'24)
   b. Part 2 (from 0'24 to 0'37)
   c. Part 3 (from 0'37 to 0'40)
   d. Part 4 (from 0'40 to 1'13)
   e. Part 5 (from 1'13 to 1'29)

3. **Use** the key information to **write** the ID card of this sport.

4. **Match** the English words with their translation.

a. a rule set — b. a field — c. to unfold — d. a feature — e. a pitcher — f. the speed — g. a batter — h. upwards — i. downwards — j. a skill — k. wit.

1. vers le bas — 2. un batteur — 3. une caractéristique — 4. une compétence — 5. se dérouler — 6. vers le haut — 7. l'intelligence / l'esprit — 8. un lanceur — 9. un règlement — 10. un terrain — 11. la vitesse

WHAT ABOUT YOU?

Do you watch Olympic Games events or other sports events? Why? Why not?

Extra Road — Vers le Bac

5. Which other information would you like to know about this sport? **Share** with your partner and **add** them to the identity card.

"The most important thing in the Olympic Games is not to win but to take part."
Pierre de Coubertin

TASK 2

PRESENTATION TIME EE / EOC Create the ID card of your favourite sport and present it to your classmates.

Challenge yourself!

My Language Challenges	J'ai des difficultés ou je réponds non…
1. Je sais exprimer la périodicité.	je fais le challenge n° 1.
2. Je suis capable de comparer deux éléments (comparatif de supériorité).	je fais le challenge n° 2.
3. Je suis capable de former un nom de personne à partir d'un verbe et de le prononcer correctement.	je fais le challenge n° 3.
4. Je sais prononcer la lettre « s » à la fin d'un mot.	je fais le challenge n° 4.

Challenge 4

Challenge 1 WORDS AND CULTURE Olympic Games Frequency

1 Take up the challenge!

Observez :

The Olympic Games take place every four years. The first ones took place in 1896. They were cancelled or postponed in 1916, 1940, 1944 and 2020.

- **Quelle est la périodicité des JO ? Quelle expression permet d'exprimer cette notion ?**
- **Quand et pourquoi ont-ils été annulés ou reportés ?**

2 Find the word!

Les JO ont lieu tous les … ans depuis 1896.

On exprime la périodicité (tous les …) avec l'expression …, complétée par le nombre d'années, de mois, de jours, d'heures, etc. qui séparent les évènements : *every three hours ; every four months ; every five years.*

Play with Words and Culture n° 2 et 3

Challenge 2 WORDS AND SENTENCES Comparisons

1 Take up the challenge!

Observez :

a. Softball fields are smaller than baseball ones.
b. Skateboarding is more spectacular than tennis.

- **Qu'expriment les expressions soulignées ?**
- **Comment se transforme l'adjectif** ***small*** **? l'adjectif** ***spectacular*** **?**
- **Comptez** le nombre de syllabes dans chaque mot en tapant dans vos mains. Que remarquez-vous ?
- **Quel mot introduit le 2ᵈ élément de comparaison ?**

2 Find the rule!

- **Pour … deux éléments entre eux**, on peut utiliser le comparatif de supériorité (+).
- **Pour les adjectifs courts** (1 syllabe), on rajoute … à l'adjectif.
- **Pour les adjectifs longs** (2 syllabes et plus), on ajoute … avant l'adjectif.
- **Dans les deux cas**, on utilise … pour introduire le 2ᵈ élément de comparaison (s'il est présent).

Attention : les adjectifs finissant par « *-y* » se transforment en « *-ier* » : *crazy* → *crazier*

Les adjectifs irréguliers : *good* → *better* / *bad* → *worse*

RECAP > p. 125
Play with Words and Sentences n° 4 et 6

Challenge 3 WORDS AND SOUNDS Words Ending with *-er*

1 Take up the challenge!

20 **Écoutez** les paires de mots et **repérez** la différence de prononciation et de sens entre les deux mots.

a. to play / a player
b. to bat / a batter
c. to score / a scorer
d. to defend / a defender

2 Find the sound!

La terminaison *-er* des mots se prononce /ə/, comme dans … .

On dit qu'il s'agit d'un son faible. C'est le son le plus fréquent en anglais britannique.

RECAP > p. 127
Play with Words and Sounds n° 11

Irregular Session

21 **Retrouvez** les trois verbes irréguliers ***throw***, ***shoot*** et ***swim*** dans le rabat à la fin du livre. **Écoutez**-les, **répétez**-les et **mémorisez**-les. **Révisez** les trois verbes appris précédemment.

3. LISTENING ROAD

Vers A2 +

Never Give up!

→ Method & Strategies

Tip 2 : Comprendre un support audio ou vidéo

VIDEO

The Best Athlete who ever lived - I am Bolt / 7.01

www.lienmini.fr/40241-14

1 **Look at** the picture. **Describe** what you see. Can you **guess** the subject of the video?

2 **Watch** the video with the *sound off*. Where and when does it take place?

3 **Watch** the video with the *sound on*. Who is this athlete and what is he famous for?

4 What are the three elements that allow the athlete to be successful according to the man with the coloured woollen cap?

5 What are the four skills required to win a gold medal according to the athlete?

Extra Road Vers le Bac

6 **Find** the three values of olympism on the Internet.

WHAT ABOUT YOU?

1 According to you, what are the other skills that an athlete must have or must develop?

2 **Look at** the wheel of sports values and **make** your top five. **Compare** with your classmates' ranking.

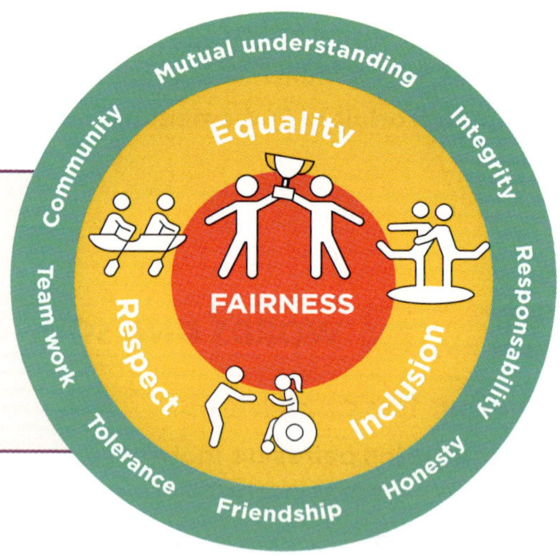

Never say never because limits, like fears, are often just an illusion.

Michael Jordan

TASK 3

FINAL MATCH EE / Médiation Create a poster listing the six most important skills and values in sports and present it.

Challenge yourself!

My Language Challenges	J'ai des difficultés ou je réponds non…
1. Je connais au moins 8 qualités et valeurs attendues d'un sportif.	je fais le challenge n° 1.
2. Je suis capable de reconnaitre et d'utiliser le superlatif.	je fais le challenge n° 2.
3. Je suis capable de repérer les différentes manières de prononcer la lettre « o ».	je fais le challenge n° 3.
4. Je sais repérer la syllabe accentuée dans un mot de deux syllabes.	je fais le challenge n° 4.

Challenge 4

Challenge 1 WORDS AND CULTURE Values

1 Take up the challenge!

Sélectionnez parmi ces noms ceux qui désignent les qualités ou valeurs attendues dans le monde du sport :

courage – fitness – energy – idleness – team spirit – balance – cheating – resistance – accuracy – unfairness – excellence

En vous appuyant sur les mots transparents et les radicaux connus, **choisissez** la traduction qui convient : courage – énergie – équilibre – esprit d'équipe – excellence – forme / aptitude – injustice – paresse / oisiveté – précision – résistance – tricherie

2 Find the word!

22 **Vérifiez** vos réponses et **mémorisez** ce lexique. **Enrichissez** votre vocabulaire en cherchant dans un dictionnaire (papier ou en ligne) les adjectifs dérivés de ces noms.

Exemple : courage → courageous.

Play with Words and Culture n° 4

Challenge 2 WORDS AND SENTENCES Superlatives

1 Take up the challenge!

Regardez attentivement les expressions soulignées. Qu'expriment-elles ?

a. This guy is without doubt <u>the greatest sprinter</u> the world has ever seen.

b. He is <u>the most impressive</u> runner in the world.

c. He is <u>the best athlete</u> who ever lived.

- **Comptez** le nombre de syllabes dans les adjectifs « *great* » et « *impressive* ». Que remarquez-vous ?
- Comment se transforment-ils ?
- Quel est le mot qui introduit ces adjectifs ?
- Quel adjectif a été transformé en « *the best* » ?

2 Find the rule!

- Pour … quelqu'un/quelque chose à un ensemble de personnes/de choses, on utilise le superlatif.
- Adjectifs courts : the + adjectif + … .
- Adjectifs longs : the + … + adjectif.

Attention : les adjectifs finissant par « *-y* » se transforment en « *-iest* » : *easy → the easiest*

Les adjectifs irréguliers : *good → the best*
bad → the worst

RECAP > p. 125
Play with Words and Sentences n° 8 et 9

Challenge 3 WORDS AND SOUNDS The Letter "o"

1 Take up the challenge!

23 **Écoutez** les mots suivants.

sport – top – score – clock – focus – short – dog – go – spot – more – most – broken

Comment se prononce la lettre « o » ?

2 Find the sound!

La lettre « o » peut se prononcer :

- /ɔ:/ comme dans … ;
- /ɒ/ comme dans … ;
- /əu/ comme dans … .

RECAP > p. 127
Play with Words and Sounds n° 12

Irregular Session

24 **Retrouvez** les trois verbes irréguliers *take*, *stand* et *lose* dans le rabat à la fin du livre. **Écoutez**-les, **répétez**-les et **mémorisez**-les. **Révisez** les six verbes appris précédemment.

Play with...

WORDS AND CULTURE

1 **Complete** the following sentences to express your tastes.

a. I think that taekwondo is very interesting, I ... this sport.

b. I ... eating sushi because it's delicious.

c. Rugby is a team sport and I used to play it. That's why I ... watching it on television.

d. Karate is too violent, I ... it.

2 **Find** where the Olympic Games took place. **Write** sentences.

Example: 1904 → The Olympic Games took place in Saint Louis, United States of America.

a. 2000

b. 1984

c. 1948

d. 2002

e. 1980

3 **Find** the translation as quickly as possible.

Tous les deux jours

Tous les trois ans

Every four weeks

Every five months

4 a. **Give** your opinion about the most important values in these sports. **Compare** with your partner's opinion.

*Example: According to me, the most important values in **judo** are **courage and ...** .*

1. **Judo:** courage, respect, modesty, friendship, honour, honesty, self-control, courtesy

2. **Basketball:** teamwork, positive attitude, honesty, hard work, effort, perseverance, fun

3. **Surfing:** endurance, energy, strength, strategy, motivation, pleasure

4. **Archery:** accuracy, power, calmness, punch, skill, determination

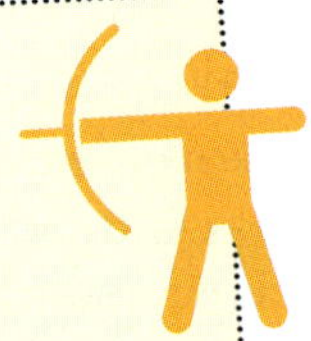

5. **Skateboarding:** boldness, resistance, agility, adaptability, anticipation, enjoyment

b. What are the athletes' qualities in each sport? **Use** adjectives.

Example: Judokas are courageous and...

c. **Compare** athletes' qualities in each sport.

Example: In judo, you have to be more respectful than courageous.

WORDS AND SENTENCES

5 **Put** the words in the right order to make sentences. **Use** capital letters when necessary.

a. do / play / tennis / you / ? /

b. practise / your parents / ? / do / a team sport /

c. your brother / which / does / sport / like / ? /

d. where / your class / meet / does / sports / to play / ? /

6 **Use** the elements to **write** sentences with a comparative.

Example: In softball games / pitchers / quick / batters. → In softball games, pitchers are quicker than batters.

a. The baseball field / large / the softball field.

b. I. / old / My classmates

c. Wrestling / dangerous / tennis.

d. Rules in softball / easy / rules in baseball.

e. His new car / cheap / mine.

f. Taekwondo is / amazing / hockey.

7 a. **Find** the title of this song by the group Daft Punk.

- ***My first is a synonym for "more difficult".***
- ***My second is the contrary to "worse".***
- ***My third is a synonym for "quicker".***

b. **Listen** to the song, **check** and **find** the adjectives.

c. **Choose** four adjectives in the superlative form and **write** the title of a song.

8 **Put** these adjectives into their superlative form.

Example: quick → the quickest

a. strong

b. motivated

c. resistant

d. light

e. courageous

9 **Transform** the adjectives in brackets into superlatives.

a. Ronaldo is ... (fast) football player in the world.

b. The London Eye is ... (impressive) tourist attraction.

c. Mister Bean is ... (funny) English series that I know.

d. Michael Jordan is ... (famous) basketball player in America.

e. I am the ... (good) player in my team.

WORDS AND SOUNDS

10 **Say** it out loud.

50% 10% 1/4 4/5

100% 2/3 30% 25%

11 In groups, **find** as many nouns as possible composed of a verb and the ending "-*er*". You've got three minutes! **Say** it out loud.

Example: to sing → a singer

3 min

12 25 a. **Listen** to the words and **associate** them with the right sound.

job - horse - no - boring - judo - so - Olympic - opera - clock - total - north - code - video

"/ɔː/ as in short"

"/əu/ as in go"

"/ɒ/ as in stop"

b. **Say** them out loud.

MISSION CONTROL

Vers A2 +

SCENARIO The IOC (International Olympic Committee) is preparing the Olympic Games for 2032. It invites young people to create a video to highlight a new sport and include it to the programme of the Olympic Games.

MISSION EOC In a one-minute video, present the popular sport you would like to add to the Olympic Games.

1. **Préparez** votre présentation :
   a. **Créez** la carte d'identité du sport que vous avez choisi.
   b. **Établissez** la liste des valeurs propres à ce sport.
   c. **Expliquez** pourquoi vous avez choisi ce sport et **comparez**-le à d'autres sports.
2. **Enregistrez** votre présentation d'une minute. **Veillez** à votre attitude devant la caméra.

KEY QUESTION Do Olympic sports reflect national or international values? What do you think now?

Assess Yourself

☺ 😐 ☹

Compétences de communication

- Présenter un sport en précisant les caractéristiques, les valeurs et les compétences attendues pour le pratiquer.
- Expliquer en quoi le sport choisi est attractif.
- Comparer un sport à un autre ou à un ensemble de sports.

Compétences linguistiques

- Connaitre et savoir prononcer le lexique du sport, ses valeurs et ses compétences.
- Connaitre les expressions de gout.
- Comprendre et utiliser le comparatif et le superlatif de supériorité.

Compétences transversales

- Comprendre et respecter la consigne.
- Organiser mon propos (introduction, plan, conclusion).
- Adopter une posture adéquate devant une caméra.

Micro Project

- Interdisciplinarité : éducation physique et sportive – parcours santé

Olympics at School

**You organise the Olympic day at your school.
Your European partners are invited.**

1 Survey Time

1. **Discuss** with your schoolmates the sports that will be proposed.
2. **Create** a survey to select the ones that will be chosen.

2 Organising the Day

- **Organise** the schedule of the day with the selected sports.

3 Announcing the Event

- **Create** a poster or a leaflet to announce the date, the place and the programme of the Olympic day.

4 Chill out!

- **Create** as many quizzes as possible for the different teams.
  Example: It's an outdoor and an indoor sport. It's played with a round ball. Players are very tall. Which sport is it?

OLYMPIC DAY
AT MY VOCATIONAL SCHOOL

22 MONDAY: Opening show at 9 am / Olympic tennis tournament at 2 pm.

23 TUESDAY: Mini Olympics : rugby and baseball from 9 am to 5 pm.

24 WEDNESDAY: Olympic day for football and volley ball from 10 am to 4 pm.

25 THURSDAY: Original Olympic day: skateboard and breakdance.

26 FRIDAY: Olympic amazing race at 1 pm / Final show at 3 pm.

Comprendre ce que je visionne

1. Identifier les stratégies

➜ **Method & Strategies**
Tip 2 : Comprendre un support audio ou vidéo

VIDEO
Chiene' Coaches to Empower | You Can't Stop Our Voice | Nike / 1'15
www.lienmini.fr/40241-15

Anticiper lors du premier visionnage

Observez le titre, la source, la date et **appuyez-vous** sur les images, la musique, le contexte, les différents interlocuteurs.

➜ Je pense que...

1 **Il s'agit d' :** a. un documentaire b. un extrait de film c. une publicité.

2 **Le document parle :** a. de basket-ball b. de tous les sports.

3 **La vidéo se déroule :** a. en Australie b. aux États-Unis c. en France d. au Royaume-Uni.

Repérer, déduire, identifier et associer lors des visionnages successifs

Lors du deuxième visionnage, repérez les noms propres, les lieux, les mots connus. **Déduisez** le sens des éléments inconnus à partir des éléments connus ou transparents.

➜ Je me pose les questions-clés (qui ? à qui ? quand ? où ? quoi ? combien ? pourquoi ?) et confirme ou infirme mes premières hypothèses.

1 **Qui ?** Chiene Joy Jones est a. une jeune basketteuse professionnelle b. un entraineur c. un top model

2 **À qui ?** Elle s'adresse à : a. des fillettes fortes, intelligentes b. des femmes acharnées, étonnantes c. de futures professionnelles affirmées.

3 **Où ?** Elle vient d'un quartier de New york : a. Bronx b. Brooklyn c. Manhattan d. Queens.

4 **Quoi ?** a. Elle a créé *Grow our Game*, un programme : **a.** sportif pour les fillettes **b.** d'entrainement pour futures professionnelles **c.** d'aide alimentaire.
b. Il offre : **a.** des séances de coaching pour les femmes des quartiers défavorisés **b.** des salles d'entrainement aux habitants de New York **c.** des activités gratuites de basket-ball pour les filles.
c. Dans sa communauté, elle est devenue : **a.** un leader **b.** un ennemi **c.** un modèle pour les jeunes filles.

5 **Pourquoi ?** Elle souhaite : a. suivre le modèle des personnes fortes qui l'entouraient b. expliquer les raisons pour lesquelles les sportifs font du sport c. rendre les jeunes filles conscientes de l'inégalité.

Lors des visionnages suivants, repérez les répétitions, les mots-clés, les marqueurs de temps. Déduisez le sens des mots inconnus. Identifiez les informations importantes.

➜ Je dégage les idées principales, les faits marquants et confirme/infirme mes hypothèses.

Chiene Joy Jones raconte ... . Elle explique que ... . Elle veut que ... .

Compléter et vérifier lors du dernier visionnage

Repérez les éléments subjectifs (adjectifs, modalité, opinion...). **Vérifiez** votre compréhension.

➜ J'identifie le point de vue et l'objectif du document.

Chiene cherche à : a. raconter b. informer c. convaincre d. dénoncer. **Le message qu'elle délivre est ... .**

2. Appliquer

En vous appuyant sur la fiche Method & Strategies n° 2 et les stratégies que vous venez de mettre en œuvre, **présentez** le document suivant.

VIDEO
Tamara Gives Back to Move Forward | You Can't Stop Our Voice | Nike / 1'15
www.lienmini.fr/40241-44

Accompagner • Ouvrir, Orienter, Oser

Oser développer mes compétences en Europe

1. Comprendre la différence entre savoir-faire et savoir-être

1 **Regardez** la vidéo et **expliquez** la différence entre les deux expressions « *hard skills* » et « *soft skills* ».

2 **Regardez** à nouveau la vidéo et **associez** chaque mot dans les séries au type de compétences correspondant. *Soft skills* ou *hard skills* ?

a. Les caractéristiques : *concrete, objective, personal, specific, required to do your work, used in every job.*

b. Les exemples : *adaptability, coding, communication, cooking, teamwork.*

c. Les moyens pour les acquérir : *naturally, previous work experience, real world, school, training.*

d. Les moyens pour les mesurer : *certification, cover letter, education, interview, on the job, previous work experience, resume.*

VIDEO
Hard Skills vs Soft Skills / 1'52
www.lienmini.fr/40241-16

TIPS

cover letter: une lettre de candidature
required: exigé
resume: un CV
teamwork: le travail d'équipe
training: la formation

2. Cibler mes savoir-faire et savoir-être

1 **Rendez-vous** sur un des sites de l'orientation du Royaume-Uni et **explorez** les différents métiers possibles en fonction de votre famille de métiers (*job family*) ou spécialité, des disciplines (*subjects*) que vous aimez ou de vos compétences (*skills*).

2 En anglais, **citez** des exemples de métiers possibles et deux compétences liées à cette famille de métiers ou spécialité.
Exemple : In the job family "catering and hospitality", there are bakers, butchers and waiters. They have good customer service skills and a good knowledge of food and drink.

3 **Choisissez**, parmi les métiers proposés, celui ou ceux que vous pourriez ou aimeriez faire.
Exemple : My main skill is teamwork. I can become a careworker or a roofer.

3. Oser

Votre correspondant vous annonce qu'il va participer au concours Euroskills. **Cherchez** sur Internet à quoi correspond ce concours et **expliquez** à votre professeur que vous aimeriez y participer l'an prochain.

a. **Donnez** des informations sur cet évènement (objectif, durée, nombre de métiers représentés, de participants, de pays participants, de visiteurs, de journalistes, type de formation concernée) et ce qu'il permet de mettre en valeur.

b. **Expliquez** pourquoi vous souhaitez participer et **indiquez** les compétences sur lesquelles vous pourriez vous appuyer à cette occasion. Pour vous aider, complétez le formulaire « My Skills Worksheet » dans votre **Bonus Road**.

UNIT 4 Job

Vers B1

- Emploi, métiers, professions, carrières
- Modalités de candidature à l'embauche

Look at the document. **Describe** what you see, **find out** where the people are and what they are doing.

YOUR ROAD MAP

www.lienmini.fr/40241-17

UP TO YOU!

- Easy Road
- Extra Road
- Bonus Road

KEY QUESTION How can job adverts help to find a job?

SCENARIO You work in a video game store during your holiday. The company organises an international youth video game contest and wants to hire webdesigners/hotliners of different nationalities.

TASK 1 JOB OFFER **EE** Answer a job offer with an email.

TASK 2 VOICE MESSAGE **EOC** Leave a voice message to give information about a company.

MISSION **EE** As part of the event's team, write a job ad and post it on the Web.

Wanted!

Open up!

TIPS

to hire: to recruit
software: un logiciel

1. What sort of document is it? **Justify.**
2. What sort of job is it about? Which material is it linked to?
3. In which type of company do you find such a job?

WHAT ABOUT YOU?

1. Have you ever read a job advertisement?
2. Have you ever answered a job offer?

Get ready!

In-Class Activities

EXERCICES
Flashcards
www.lienmini.fr/40241-18

1. a. **Look at** the words on the flashcards. **Listen** and **repeat**.
   b. **Look at** the translations and **try to** remember the English words.
2. When possible, **find** in the list:
   a. words with the same radical.
   b. synonyms.
   c. antonyms.
3. **CHAIN SPEAKING Repeat** a word of the series. Then one of your classmates repeats it and adds another one. **Go** as far as possible in the series.

By yourself!

Find out what the ordinary working hours are for an employee in the UK.

Come for the Job!

Front Desk Overnight Receptionist

TownePlace Suites by Marriott Rochester, MN 55901

- Job type: Part-time
- Benefits*: Employee discount / Paid time off
- Education: High school or equivalent (Preferred)
- Typical start time: 11 PM
- Pay: $12.00 - $14.00 per hour
- Schedule: 8-hour shift* / Night shift / Weekends
- Hours per week: 10-19
- Typical end time: 7 AM
- Administrative duties: Stocking supplies / Answering and routing phone calls / Greeting visitors
- Financial duties: Processing payments
- Age condition: You must be over 18 to apply for this job offer.
- Hard skills required: You must have written and verbal communication skills. You must be familiar with Microsoft Office.
- Soft skills required: Dependability, Problem-solving, Ability to work under pressure, Attention to detail
- Company's website: www.marriott.com/rstts
- Work remotely*: No

If you require alternative methods of application or screening, you must approach the employer directly to request this as Indeed *is not responsible for the employer's application process.*

Adapted from www.indeed.com

TIPS
benefit: un avantage
shift: une équipe, un poste
remotely: à distance

→ Method & Strategies
Tip 3 : Comprendre un support écrit

1. **Observe** the document. What sort of document is it?
2. **Look at** the headline and **choose** the right information.
   a. The job is about: welcoming clients / cooking meals / repairing computers.
   b. It is in: a vocational school / a hospital / a hotel.
3. **Read** the different items and **answer** the questions with full sentences.
   a. In which town is the job offered? **Give the name of the country and the state.**
   b. How much can you earn per hour?
   c. Is it a full-time or a part-time job?
   d. What are the working hours?
   e. What are the benefits offered by the company?

WHAT ABOUT YOU?

Would you like to do this job? to work in this country? **Explain** and **list** the pros and cons with your classmates.

Extra Road — Vers le Bac

4. **Find out** the essential duties and the required skills to work as a receptionist.
5. Are there shifts in an office? In a car factory? **Make research** if necessary and **draw** a list of jobs with a possible shift pattern (mornings, afternoons, nights) with your classmates.

> *The only way to do great work is to love what you do. If you haven't found it yet, keep looking. Don't settle.*
>
> *Steve Jobs*

TASK 1

JOB OFFER EE Answer the job offer with an email.

Give your qualities and your professional skills. **Remember** words from **UNIT 2** and **UNIT 3**.

Challenge yourself!

My Language Challenges	J'ai des difficultés ou je réponds non…
1. Je comprends les rubriques d'une offre d'emploi.	je fais le challenge n° 1.
2. Je sais exprimer l'obligation et l'interdiction avec « *must* ».	je fais le challenge n° 2.
3. Je sais prononcer la lettre « y ».	je fais le challenge n° 3.
4. Je sais distinguer la prononciation anglaise et américaine de certains mots (« *schedule* », « *advertisement* », « *mobile* »…).	je fais le challenge n° 4.

Challenge 4

Challenge 1 WORDS AND CULTURE Components of a Job Ad

1 Take up the challenge!

Dans quel type de document trouve-t-on les expressions suivantes ?

education – benefits – **schedule** – pay –
job type – job title – duties – required skills

2 Find the word!

Mémorisez le nom des rubriques des offres d'emploi. **Cherchez** et **associez** chacune des rubriques en gras avec 2 à 3 mots correspondant à votre famille ou à votre corps de métier. **Mémorisez**-les.

Play with Words and Culture n° 1 et 5

Challenge 2 WORDS AND SENTENCES Obligation

1 Take up the challenge!

Observez :

a. You <u>must</u> approach the employer.
b. You <u>must</u> be over 18.
c. You <u>mustn't</u> be late for a job interview.

- **Qu'exprime l'auxiliaire de modalité souligné ?**
- **Où se place-t-il par rapport au verbe et au sujet ?**

2 Find the rule!

- **Pour exprimer une …, j'utilise le modal *must*. Il se place entre le … et la … .**
- **Pour exprimer une interdiction, j'utilise *mustn't*.**

RECAP > p. 125
Play with Words and Sentences n° 6 et 7

Challenge 3 WORDS AND SOUNDS The Letter "y"

1 Take up the challenge!

26 **Écoutez** les mots suivants :

a type – a payment – a day – to apply – to employ – typical – remotely

La prononciation de la lettre « y » est-elle identique pour chaque mot ?

2 Find the sound!

La lettre « y » peut se prononcer :

- /aɪ/comme dans … ;
- /i/ comme dans … .

Ou dans des sons composés :

- /eɪ/ comme dans … ;
- /ɔɪ/ comme dans … .

RECAP > p. 127
Play with Words and Sounds n° 9

Irregular Session

27 **Retrouvez** les trois verbes irréguliers ***bring***, ***have*** et ***tell*** dans le rabat à la fin du livre. **Écoutez**-les, **répétez**-les et **mémorisez**-les.

2. LISTENING ROAD

Vers B1

This Is my Company!

VIDEO Working for TPP / 2'02
www.lienmini.fr/40241-19

➔ Method & Strategies
Tip 2 : Comprendre un support audio ou vidéo

1. **Look at** the freeze frame above and **watch** the video *sound off*. **Describe** what you see and **guess** what the video is about.

2. **Watch** the video *sound on*. **Pay attention** to the places, the words you know and the stressed words to **answer** these questions.
   a. What type of company is it?
   b. Where is the company located (country, county, city)?
   c. What does the company provide to its clients? Who are they?

3. **Watch the video again.**
   a. **Match the key words you hear (1) with their translation (2).**
   1. software – healthcare – GP surgeries – customers – experience – pricing – sailing
   2. clients – expérience – cabinets médicaux – logiciels – navigation – soins de santé – tarif
   b. **Select the adjectives you hear.**
   flexible – rigid – encouraged – discouraged – friendly – unfriendly – willing – reluctant – vibrant – dull – abundant – empty

TIPS
IT: information technology
GP: general practitioner (un médecin généraliste)
uni : university

WHAT ABOUT YOU?
Would you like to work for the company TPP? For another company? **Give** your reasons.

Extra Road Vers le Bac

4. **Find** at least: one reason why starting working in this company is interesting, two positive aspects in its location and three pieces of information about the working environment.

5. What elements could be added in the TPP company presentation? **Find** them on the company's website and **compare** your answers to your classmates'.

> *“The future belongs to those who believe in the beauty of their dreams.”*
> *Eleanor Roosevelt*

TASK 2

VOICE MESSAGE EOC Leave a voice message to give information about a company.

Your friend has seen a job ad and asks your opinion about the company.

1. **Search** the Internet and **find** an interesting job ad.
2. **Look** for information about the company.
3. **Leave** a voice message on your friend's answering machine to **tell** him/her about the information you have found.
4. **Give** your opinion about it.

Challenge yourself!

My Language Challenges	J'ai des difficultés ou je réponds non…
1. Je sais reconnaitre et lire un nom composé.	je fais le challenge n° 1.
2. Je sais choisir entre l'article « *the* » et l'article zéro.	je fais le challenge n° 2.
3. Je suis capable de lire et de prononcer des acronymes.	je fais le challenge n° 3.
4. Je sais situer la ville de Leeds et j'en connais quelques caractéristiques.	**je fais le challenge n° 4.**

Challenge 4

Challenge 1 WORDS AND CULTURE Compound Nouns

1 Take up the challenge!

Observez les noms composés suivants :

a software company - a world-class IT healthcare system - the training approaches

- Quel mot désigne l'objet ou la personne dont il est question ? Où est-il placé ?
- **Traduisez** ces noms composés.

2 Find the word!

Pour comprendre un nom composé, on se concentre d'abord sur le … nom.

Les autres noms donnent des informations sur ce mot.

Play with Words and Culture n° 2

Challenge 2 WORDS AND SENTENCES "The" or "Ø"?

1 Take up the challenge!

Observez les noms soulignés :

a. Half of the GP surgeries in the UK are using our software. / The job can be challenging.

b. It transforms healthcare. / You can ask for help. / You are working with people.

Comparez :

- Quel article précède les noms soulignés ?
- Quelle est la différence entre les deux séries de noms ?

2 Find the rule!

- On utilise l'article … pour désigner une personne, un objet, un évènement précis et défini.
- Quand un nom représente une notion abstraite ou une généralité, on supprime cet article. On dit qu'on utilise l'article zéro.

RECAP > p. 125
Play with Words and Sentences n° 8

Challenge 3 WORDS AND SOUNDS Computers and Acronyms

1 Take up the challenge!

28 **Écoutez** les acronymes suivants :

HTTPS - www - PC - IT - AI - RAM

- **Répétez**-les et **mémorisez**-les.
- **Cherchez** leur signification.

2 Find the sound!

Il existe des acronymes pour chaque domaine d'activité.

Trouvez d'autres acronymes anglais et **vérifiez** leur prononciation.

Play with Words and Sounds n° 11 et 12

Irregular Session

29 **Retrouvez** les trois verbes irréguliers ***pay***, ***sit*** et ***understand*** dans le rabat à la fin du livre.
Écoutez-les, **répétez**-les et **mémorisez**-les. **Révisez** les trois verbes appris précédemment.

Play with...

WORDS AND CULTURE

1 Find the odd ones.

a. pay rate / marital status / location / skills / height / weight / qualities

b. ad / vacation / health insurance / shift / early retirement / application / sick leave / child care

c. problem-solving / teamwork / beauty / initiative / strength / planning / dependability

2 Form teams of three or four. Write the French translation of these compound nouns. The winner is the fastest team.

employment type – contract type – working hours – recruiter type – job title – application process – pay rate – software developer – part-time job – health insurance – phone call

3 a. **Situate Leeds on a map. Is it in the north, south, east or west of the country?**

b. **Look at a road planning website and find the distance in miles and in kilometres between Leeds and London, between Leeds and Manchester.**

c. **How far is Leeds from the Scottish border (from Lamberton, a Scottish border town, for example)?**

4 Look for information about Leeds and check if the following facts are right or wrong.

a. Leeds is in Scotland.

b. Leeds has 5 universities.

c. The river Thames flows through the city of Leeds.

d. Leeds has an oceanic climate.

e. Leeds United is the name of the football team.

f. There are over 16 museums in Leeds.

5 Match the information with the corresponding items of the job offer.

job – pay – benefits – schedule – education – experience – hours per week – age condition – soft skills – work remotely

Job Offer

a. You must be over 18.

b. Part-time nanny job.

c. Being great with kids.

d. £9-£12 per hour.

e. Afternoon hours.

f. High school or equivalent.

g. Paid-time off, free online paediatric first aid training (if required), extra 50p per hour after 6 months, another extra 50p per hour after 12 months.

h. Up to 15 hours.

i. Previous experience looking after children is essential.

j. No work remotely.

WORDS AND SENTENCES

6 Complete with *must* or *mustn't*.

a. As a brick-layer, I ... wear my personal protective equipment.

b. You ... drink alcohol during your work placement in this IT factory.

c. At the hotel reception, you ... be polite and smiling.

d. I'm 13, I ... drive my parents' car in the city.

e. The workers ... respect the company's safety rules.

7 Translate into English. Use *must* or *mustn't*.

a. Je dois être ponctuel pendant ma période de formation en entreprise.

b. Les apprentis ne doivent pas utiliser leur téléphone portable pendant leur travail.

c. Les candidats doivent apporter leur CV.

d. Tu dois être sociable avec les clients.

8 Complete with "*the*" if necessary.

a. I like ... milk and ... honey but I hate ... wine.

b. Do you know ... new president of ... United States?

c. I have just listened to ... last song by Beyoncé.

d. On ... Sundays, I enjoy walking in the forests.

e. Have you read ... famous book about French recipes?

f. My sister isn't keen on ... chocolate.

WORDS AND SOUNDS

9 a. **Say the words out loud.**

to pay - an employer - to supply - directly - dynamic - today - to buy - to identify - a company

b. **Match them with the right pronunciation of the letter "y".**

"/aɪ/" "/i/" "/eɪ/"

or

"/ɔɪ/"

10 (30) **Listen** to the words, **repeat** them and **say if they are pronounced with a British or an American accent.**

data - status - schedule - tomato - water

11 **Form** teams of three or four.

a. **Read the expressions.**

Central Processing Unit - Internet Protocol - Virtual Private Network - Local Area Network - Power-On Self-Test

b. **Take the first letters of each word to build the acronyms used in the IT field.**

c. **Say them out loud.**

You've got three minutes to play!

12 **Search** the Internet, **find what these acronyms stand for in video games and say them aloud.**

ARPG

SIM

MMO

TMG

RPG

HOG

MISSION CONTROL

Vers B1

SCENARIO You work in a video game store during your holiday. The company organises an international youth video game contest and wants to hire webdesigners/hotliners of different nationalities.

MISSION EE As part of the event's team, write a job ad and post it on the Web.

1 Par deux, **imaginez** les caractéristiques de l'entreprise qui recrute et **listez** :
- a. les informations importantes relatives à l'entreprise et au projet ;
- b. les tâches, les compétences et les qualités attendues pour l'emploi proposé ;
- c. les caractéristiques de l'emploi proposé (salaire, horaires, niveau d'études...) ;
- d. les avantages que l'entreprise pourra offrir ;
- e. les conditions nécessaires pour accéder au poste (âge minimum, permis de conduire, date de disponibilité...).

2 Rédigez ensuite individuellement votre annonce.
- a. **Écrivez** un petit paragraphe d'introduction pour présenter le projet et souligner le dynamisme de votre entreprise.
- b. **Organisez** les rubriques de l'offre d'emploi.
- c. **Finissez** votre annonce en rédigeant une ou deux phrases précisant les conditions à respecter. **Utilisez** l'expression d'obligation étudiée.

KEY QUESTION How can job adverts help to find a job? What do you think now?

Assess Yourself

	🙂	😐	🙁
Compétences de communication			
→ Indiquer les caractéristiques et attendus d'une offre d'emploi.			
→ Présenter une entreprise (implantation, secteur d'activité, pays partenaires...).			
→ Préciser les avantages offerts au sein d'une entreprise.			
Compétences linguistiques			
→ Connaitre et utiliser le lexique lié aux offres d'emplois.			
→ Savoir employer l'article zéro ou l'article « *the* ».			
→ Exprimer une obligation.			
Compétences transversales			
→ Comprendre et respecter la consigne.			
→ Organiser mon écrit.			
→ Respecter la présentation d'une offre d'emploi.			

Exam Road

COMPRÉHENSION DE L'ORAL

CE
EOC-EOI

VIDEO
Indeed Job Search Tips / 1'14
www.lienmini.fr/40241-20

Visionnez cette vidéo trois fois et **choisissez** les bonnes réponses.

1 **De quel type de vidéo s'agit-il ?**
a. un spot publicitaire concernant les difficultés pour trouver un métier
b. un tuto donnant des astuces pour rechercher un travail sur Internet
c. une vidéo apportant des conseils pour un entretien d'embauche

2 **Le nom du site est :**
a. Headed b. Monstered c. Indeed

3 **Quelle est la première étape à suivre ?**
a. inscrire l'intitulé précis du métier recherché et le nom de l'entreprise dans laquelle vous souhaitez travailler b. écrire une lettre de motivation c. attendre une confirmation

4 **Quelle autre information peut être précisée ?**
a. les personnes avec lesquelles vous souhaitez travailler b. la distance maximale entre l'entreprise et le domicile c. les horaires que vous refusez

5 **Votre demande a plus de chance d'être vue par l'employeur si :**
a. vous fermez les vidéos en cours. b. vous inscrivez cette annonce dans votre agenda. c. vous postulez dès la parution de l'offre d'emploi.

6 **Quel est le point de vue de la présentatrice ?**
a. Les petits changements sont parfois les plus intelligents. b. Qui dort dine. c. Aux grands maux les grands remèdes.

→ Vers le Bac **À partir de vos éléments de réponse, rédigez un compte-rendu en français du support. Vous préciserez la nature et le thème principal, les informations importantes, ainsi que la fonction du document.**

EXPRESSION ÉCRITE

Vous traiterez, en anglais et en 80 mots minimum, le sujet suivant.

Rappel : l'attendu au baccalauréat sera de 100 à 120 mots.

Sujet :

You have received this message from your best friend John. Write a message to answer.

Hi! How are you doing? I need your help. I want to work next summer. Can you give me some advice to write my job offer? Thanks. See you. John

Accompagner ● Personnaliser

Comprendre ce que je lis

→ Method & Strategies
Tip 3 : Comprendre un support écrit

What's not to like?* Work one hour a day, get paid $85,000

By Andy Thompson Appleton Post-Crescent – October 22, 2020

An attractive — and lucrative — job offer showed up in my email last week. I was being recruited for an account manager position at a steel company. I'd be responsible for managing the company's accounts receivable in the U.S.
Here's the pitch: "We decided to contact you to see if you are interested in the position, this is a one-year contract with a 10% commission, a salary of $5,000 per month and $25,000 after the contract expires, the time required for this task is less than 1 hour per day. Please respond and let us know if you are interested in the position."
Work one hour a day, make $85,000 in a year and get a sales commission? Can't get much better than that. Never mind that I know as much about accounts receivable as I do about quantum physics. Or that I wasn't looking for a new job.
This was one of the more obvious scams I've seen in a long time. It ranks right up there on the ridiculous scale with the "pay your IRS* tax penalty now or we'll have you arrested" and "we need access to your computer to fix a problem."

https://eu.postcrescent.com

TIP
IRS or Internal Revenue Service: les autorités fiscales aux États-Unis
What's not to like: il a tout pour plaire

1. Identifier les stratégies

Anticiper avant la première lecture

Observez le titre et le paratexte. **Mobilisez** vos connaissances et vos acquis.

→ Je pense que…

1. **Il s'agit de :** a. un message b. un récit c. une offre d'emploi d. un article de journal
2. **Le document parle :** a. des conditions de travail b. d'arnaques c. de passe-temps

Repérer, déduire, identifier et associer lors des différentes lectures

Lors de la première lecture, **repérez** les noms propres, les indications chiffrées, les sigles, les mots connus. **Déduisez** le sens des éléments inconnus à partir des éléments connus ou transparents.

→ Je me pose les questions clés et choisis les hypothèses correctes :

1. **Qui ?** a. le président des États-Unis b. une entreprise sidérurgique c. le contrôleur des impôts
2. **Quand ?** a. le 22 octobre 2020 b. la semaine suivante c. la semaine précédente d. le jour précédent
3. **Quoi ?** a. une offre d'emploi réelle b. une offre d'emploi fictive c. une demande d'emploi fictive
4. **Où ?** a. dans sa boite aux lettres b. sur sa messagerie téléphonique c. sur sa messagerie électronique
5. **Quelles données chiffrées ?** a. le salaire mensuel b. le salaire annuel c. la prime d'assurance d. des impôts e. une commission sur les ventes f. le nombre d'heures de travail par jour

Lors des lectures suivantes, **repérez** les répétitions, les champs lexicaux, les mots-clés, les marqueurs de temps, la ponctuation. Mettez en relation les informations importantes.

→ Je dégage les idées principales, les faits marquants et confirme/infirme mes hypothèses :

Le journaliste raconte … . Il explique que … . Il questionne … . Il déduit que … et donne des exemples : … .

Compléter et vérifier lors de la dernière lecture

Repérez les éléments subjectifs. **Vérifiez** votre compréhension.

→ J'identifie le point de vue de l'auteur et l'objectif du document :

Le journaliste donne son opinion sur … . Il veut : a. informer b. divertir c. dénoncer.

2. Appliquer

En vous appuyant sur la fiche Method & strategies n° 3 et les stratégies que vous venez de mettre en œuvre, **présentez** le document proposé dans votre Bonus Road.

S'exprimer sur les compétences et qualités sportives et professionnelles

Irregular Fight

1. Guessing Games

Soyez plus rapide que votre camarade en trouvant le sport ou le métier correspondant aux définitions suivantes. Chaque définition vaut 1 point. Le premier qui marque 3 points a gagné.

a. you play it outdoor / it's very popular in America, Canada and Asia / it is played with a bat /

b. you work indoor or outdoor / you lead actors and actresses / you are in charge of the technicians

c. you play it outdoor / it's a very technical sport / you need clubs to play / some famous presidents practice it

d. you work indoor and outdoor / you wear original clothes made by fashion designers / you are tall / it's a masculine and feminine job

e. you play it alone or in groups / you don't need any ball or bat / you just need your body and music

2. Race Against the Clock!

2 min

1 **Lisez** les mots suivants et **dites** s'il s'agit de défauts ou de qualités. Vous avez 2 minutes !

motivation – honesty – arrogance – strength – fair play – vanity – jealousy – strategy – courage – determination – humility – laziness – excessive pride – calmness – selfishness – self-control – commitment – respect – friendship – resistance – cheating – vulgarity – energy

2 31 **Vérifiez** votre prononciation.

3. Ready to Debate?

Formez deux équipes et **débattez** en anglais sur le sujet suivant. Chaque équipe défendra un point de vue en utilisant des arguments pour convaincre l'équipe adverse.

Olympic Games don't attract young spectators any more.

Help

Older adults are attracted. / Athletes use social media to share Olympic moments. / New sports like skateboarding or breakdance are proposed. / There are online games about Olympic Games. / There are a lot of job opportunities for young people. / A lot of young people don't feel concerned. / Olympic Games are shown on TV, not online...

4. What Is the Truth?

Les faits énoncés dans les phrases suivantes sont-ils vrais ou faux ? **Effectuez** des recherches sur Internet si besoin et **corrigez** si nécessaire.

a. At the age of 10, Dimitrios Loundras is the youngest recorded athlete at an Olympic Games event.

b. At the age of 72, Oscar Swahn is the oldest athlete to compete in an Olympic event.

c. Michael Phelps is the most decorated Olympian of all time.

d. Usain Bolt is the world's fastest man.

e. Simone Biles is the most decorated female runner in the history of the Olympics.

5. Be a Good Sportsman/woman and a Good Professional

3 min

1 En équipe, **trouvez** les qualités nécessaires pour être un bon sportif. Vous avez 3 minutes. L'équipe qui trouve le plus de qualités a gagné.

2 De la même façon, **jouez** pour trouver les qualités qui caractérisent un bon professionnel.

UNIT 5 History

Vers B1

- Jours fériés et fêtes nationales
- Emblèmes, drapeaux, hymnes

Look at the document and describe what you see. Guess what the people are celebrating.

YOUR ROAD MAP

www.lienmini.fr/40241-21

UP TO YOU!

- Easy Road
- Extra Road
- Bonus Road

KEY QUESTION How does the national day reflect the culture of a country?

SCENARIO The language assistant of your school presents the celebration of the national day in her country.

TASK 1 BE A JOURNALIST **EE** Write a short article to present the American national day.

TASK 2 PRESENTATION TIME **EOC** Give information about the English national day.

TASK 3 ONCE UPON A TIME... IN THE WORLD **EOI** / **Médiation** Present and compare the national day of 3 English-speaking countries.

MISSION **CO** / **EOC** / **Médiation** Listen to the language assistant's presentation, present the national day in your country and explain the similarities and differences between the two celebrations.

and Stories

Open up!

Look at the picture.

1. What sort of document is it?
2. Which country is it about? **List** the different symbols which refer to that country.
3. **Read** the slogan.
   a. Which celebration is this card for?
   b. Referring to movies or TV series you know, **give** another name for this celebration.

WHAT ABOUT YOU?

1. What's the date of the national day in the country you are from?
2. Can you list symbols which refer to your own country?

Get ready!

In-Class Activities

EXERCICES
Flashcards
www.lienmini.fr/40241-22

1. **Look at** the flashcards. **Listen to** the words and **repeat**.
2. **Memorise** the way the words are written.
3. 32 **Listen to** the word and **write** the number corresponding to the picture. Then **write** the word.

	number	word

	1	fireworks

By yourself!

WORD CLOUD Use the words of the USA symbols and **create** a word cloud representing one of the emblems of the USA.

Stars, Stripes and Fireworks

➔ Method & Strategies
Tip 2 : Comprendre un support audio ou vidéo

TIP
cookouts: *cook* (cuisiner) + *out* (à l'extérieur)
➔ des barbecues

VIDEO
What is Independence Day? / 1'05
www.lienmini.fr/40241-23

1 **Watch** the video and **pay attention** to what you can see or hear. **Answer** the following questions.
a. What type of background sound can you hear?
b. How many characters are speaking?
c. What type of visual elements can you see?
d. What sort of video is it?

2 **Watch** the video **again** and **put** these titles in the order they appear in the video.
country – date of celebration – historic event – name – symbols of celebration

3 **Listen again** and **pay attention to** the details. **Find out** and **write** as much information as you can about each title.

4 **Discuss** with your classmates to complete your information.

Extra Road Vers le Bac

5 John Adams was the second president of the United States. **Search** the Internet to find who was the first one. Do you know any other famous presidents?

6 **Complete** the timeline in the Bonus Road with the most famous presidents.

WHAT ABOUT YOU?

Listen to the last question in the video. **Imagine** you're an American student and **answer** it.

"Ask not what your country can do for you, ask what you can do for your country."
John F. Kennedy

TASK 1

BE A JOURNALIST EE Write a short article to present the American national day.
With the different elements from the identity card (see Annex p. 113), **write** a short article (about 50 words) about the American national day.

Challenge yourself!

My Language Challenges	J'ai des difficultés ou je réponds non...
1. Je connais l'histoire de l'indépendance des États-Unis et je sais lire / prononcer les années correspondantes.	je fais le challenge n° 1.
2. Je suis capable de conjuguer au prétérit (ou *simple past*) à la forme affirmative.	je fais le challenge n° 2.
3. Je sais prononcer la terminaison « *-ed* » du prétérit des verbes réguliers.	je fais le challenge n° 3.
4. Je connais deux façons de dire « histoire », « anniversaire » et « maison ».	je fais le challenge n° 4.

Challenge 4

Challenge 1 WORDS AND CULTURE The Independence of the USA

1 Take up the challenge!

Retrouvez l'évènement historique correspondant à chaque date. 1492 - 1620 - 1776 - 1783

a. Arrival of British people in America.

b. Discovery of America by Christopher Columbus.

c. Election of George Washington, the first American president.

d. Declaration of Independence.

- **Lisez** ces dates à haute voix. Que remarquez-vous ?

2 Find the word!

- Pour lire une année, on lit d'abord ... puis ... .

Attention : 1905 → Nineteen o five
2020 → twenty twenty

- Après la découverte du continent par ... en 1492, les premiers colons, originaires de ... arrivent en Amérique. La révolution américaine, aussi appelée guerre ... , mène à la création d'un pays indépendant en ... . George Washington est le 1er président américain élu en ... .

Play with Words and Culture n° 5

Challenge 2 WORDS AND SENTENCES Simple Past

1 Take up the challenge!

Observez :

a. On July the 4th, 1776, the Congress adopted the Declaration of Independence.

b. This was the birth of the United States.

- **Relevez** les verbes des phrases ci-dessus.
- **Indiquez** leur infinitif et **comparez**-le avec la forme conjuguée. Que remarquez-vous ?
- **Repérez** l'indicateur de temps. Quel temps est utilisé ?

→ FLAP: 92 Useful Irregular Verbs

2 Find the rule!

Lorsqu'une action est passée, datée et terminée, on utilise le ... .

À la forme affirmative, on ajoute ... à la base verbale (infinitif sans *to*) pour les verbes réguliers.

Le prétérit des verbes irréguliers est indiqué dans la ... colonne de la liste des verbes irréguliers.

To be devient ... avec les sujets *I*, *she*, *he*, *it* ou ... avec les sujets *we*, *you*, *they*.

RECAP > p. 125
Play with Words and Sentences n° 6 et 7

Challenge 3 WORDS AND SOUNDS *-ed* Pronunciation

1 Take up the challenge!

33 **Écoutez** ces verbes et **classez-les** selon la prononciation du « *-ed* » final.

signed - celebrated - looked - enjoyed - needed - watched - commemorated

Quelles sont les lettres qui précèdent « *-ed* » dans la prononciation en /id/ ?

/t/

/d/

/id/

2 Find the sound!

Le « *-ed* » du prétérit se prononce de 3 manières : ... ou ... ou ... .

Attention : il ne se prononce **jamais** /ed/.
Si « *-ed* » est précédé de la lettre ... ou ..., il se prononcera /id/.

RECAP > p. 127
Play with Words and Sounds n° 11

Irregular Session

34 **Retrouvez** les trois verbes irréguliers *sing*, *burn* et *win* dans le rabat à la fin du livre. **Écoutez**-les, **répétez**-les et **mémorisez**-les.

Keep Calm and Celebrate!

St George's Day in the United Kingdom

St George's Day in England remembers St George, England's patron saint. The anniversary of his death, which is on April 23, is seen as England's national day. According to legend, he was a soldier in the Roman army who killed a dragon and saved a princess.

Public life: St. George's Day is not a public holiday. Businesses have normal opening hours. Schools, stores, post offices, businesses and other organisations are open as usual. Public transport services run to their usual timetables.

About St George's Day: St George is most widely known for slaying* a dragon. According to legend, the only well* in the town of Silene was guarded by a dragon. In order to get water, the inhabitants of the town had to offer a human sacrifice every day to the dragon. The person to be sacrificed was chosen by lots. On the day that St George was visiting, a princess had been selected to be sacrificed. However, he killed the dragon, saved the princess and gave the people of Silene access to water. In gratitude, they converted to Christianity.

Symbols: The most widely recognised symbol of St George's Day is St George's cross. This is a red cross on a white background, which is often displayed as a flag. It is used as England's national flag, forming part of the Union Flag, the national flag of the United Kingdom of Great Britain and Northern Ireland.

Adapted from https://www.timeanddate.com

TIPS
to slay: tuer
a well: un puits

1. **Look at** the picture. What do you think the text is about?

2. **Read** the introduction and the title of the different parts. What sort of information will you find in the text?

3. a. Now **read** the text and **answer** the following questions.
   1. What is the name of this celebration?
   2. Where does it take place?
   3. When is it celebrated?
   4. What is its origin?
   5. What is its main symbol?
   6. Is this celebration a public holiday? **Justify**.

   b. **Match** the 6 questions above with the type of information they correspond to.
   date of celebration - origin - symbol - country - name - public holiday or working day

   c. **Create** an identity card for this celebration.

→ Method & Strategies
Tip 3 : Comprendre un support écrit

WHAT ABOUT YOU?

1. Do you know another name for the Union flag?
2. How do you celebrate your own national day?

Extra Road — Vers le Bac

4. What is the link between the English flag and the flag of the United Kingdom?

5. 🎧 35 **Listen** and **say** how St George's day is celebrated in England today.

> *"Success is the ability to go from one failure to another with no loss of enthusiasm."*
> Winston Churchill

TASK 2

PRESENTATION TIME EOC Give information about the English national day.

You have one minute to present the English national day. **Give** as much information as possible. Don't forget to use the identity card.

Challenge yourself!

My Language Challenges	J'ai des difficultés ou je réponds non...
1. Je connais au moins 4 services publics, 4 lieux de loisirs et 4 commerces.	je fais le challenge n° 1.
2. Je suis capable d'introduire les dates avec la bonne préposition.	je fais le challenge n° 2.
3. Je connais les pays et les capitales formant les iles Britanniques et je sais les prononcer correctement.	je fais le challenge n° 3.
4. Je connais les symboles des pays qui composent les iles Britanniques.	je fais le challenge n° 4.

Challenge 4

Challenge 1 WORDS AND CULTURE Shops and Facilities

1 Take up the challenge!

Lisez attentivement cet extrait du texte :

St. George's Day is not a public holiday. Businesses have normal opening hours. Schools, stores, post offices, businesses and other organisations are open as usual. Public transport services run to their usual timetables.

- Qu'est-ce que « *a public holiday* » ?
- **Listez** en anglais les lieux qui sont habituellement fermés ce jour-là et ceux qui restent ouverts.

2 Find the word!

A ..., aussi appelé *bank holiday* ou *national holiday*, est un jour férié.

Certains services publics et sociétés privées sont habituellement fermés. *Exemples : schools*, ..., ..., ...

D'autres restent ouverts. *Exemples :* ..., ..., ...

Play with Words and Culture n° 1, 2 et 3

Challenge 2 WORDS AND SENTENCES Giving Dates

1 Take up the challenge!

Observez :

a. St George's Day is on April 23rd.

b. The Declaration of Independence was signed in 1776 in the USA.

c. The French and the American national days both take place in July.

- **Relevez** les dates dans chacune des phrases ci-dessus.
- Quelles prépositions les introduisent ?

2 Find the rule!

Pour introduire une date, on ajoute la préposition :

- ... pour indiquer une année ;
- ... pour indiquer un mois ;
- ... pour indiquer un jour précis.

RECAP > p. 125
Play with Words and Sentences n° 8 et 9

Challenge 3 WORDS AND SOUNDS The British Isles

1 Take up the challenge!

36 a. **Écoutez** et **répétez** les noms des pays.

1. Great Britain = England + Scotland + Wales.
2. The UK = Great Britain + Northern Ireland.
3. The British Isles = the UK + the Republic of Ireland (or Eire).

37 b. **Écoutez** et **répétez** les noms des capitales.

London – Edinburgh – Cardiff – Dublin – Belfast

2 Find the sound!

À l'oral, **associez** les capitales aux pays.

Vérifiez votre prononciation.

→ FLAP: English-Speaking Countries

Irregular Session

38 **Retrouvez** les trois verbes irréguliers *give*, *run* et *do* dans le rabat à la fin du livre.
Écoutez-les, **répétez**-les et **mémorisez**-les. **Révisez** les trois verbes appris précédemment.

Be Free, Live Free, Feel Free!

→ Method & Strategies
Tip 2 : Comprendre un support audio ou vidéo

VIDEO
Know your History: Freedom Day / 1'19
www.lienmini.fr/40241-24

1 **Watch** the video with the *sound off*.
a. **Focus on** the colours used in the video: what can you notice? Which event does the transition between the two types of colours show?
b. **Look at** the flag at the end of the video. **Guess** which country it is about. Who is the famous person delivering speeches?

2 **Watch** the video with the *sound on*.
a. **Give** the date which is repeated. What happened on that date?
b. **Find** a synonym for *segregation*.
c. **Find out** who won the election in 1994. Why is this date such a historical event?
d. **Look at** the newspaper the woman is reading while queuing. **Guess** the name of the national day commemorated every April 27 in that country.

3 **Write** the identity card of this national day. **Compare** it with your partner's.

WHAT ABOUT YOU?

1 Do you know any country where there is more than one official language? Do you know why?

2 Do you speak fluently more than one language? Which ones?

Extra Road Vers le Bac

4 **Look at** the street posters in the black and white part of the video.
a. What do they refer to?
b. In which languages are they written?

5 **Search** on the Internet the reason why there are 2 languages in these posters.

"I never lose, I either win or learn."
Nelson Mandela

TASK 3

ONCE UPON A TIME... IN THE WORLD EOI / *Médiation* **Present and compare the national day of 3 English-speaking countries.**

1 **Get into** groups of 3. Each of you in the group represents one of these 3 countries: the United States of America, England or South Africa.

2 **Give** information about its national day, **listen to** your partners, then **discuss** and **compare**. **Go on** until you have presented all the information you know. **Do not forget to** use linking words to compare.

Challenge yourself!

My Language Challenges	J'ai des difficultés ou je réponds non...
1. Je connais les mots de liaison pour indiquer un contraste ou une similitude.	je fais le challenge n° 1.
2. Je suis capable de construire des phrases avec les pronoms relatifs *who* et *which*.	je fais le challenge n° 2.
3. Je suis capable de prononcer les mots en « *-ism* ».	je fais le challenge n° 3.
4. Je connais l'histoire de l'apartheid en Afrique du Sud.	je fais le challenge n° 4.

Challenge 4

Challenge 1 WORDS AND CULTURE Linking Words

1 Take up the challenge!

Observez :

a. While there were threats of political violence, the election took place peacefully.

b. Similarly to Martin Luther King in the USA, Nelson Mandela fought against segregation in South Africa.

Précisez si ces phrases indiquent un contraste ou une similitude.

- Quel mot de liaison est utilisé pour chacune de ces deux notions ?
- Connaissez-vous d'autres mots pour indiquer le contraste ?

2 Find the word!

- Pour indiquer un ..., on peut utiliser des mots de liaison comme *but* (mais), *yet* (cependant), *whereas* (alors que), *on the contrary* (au contraire), *however* (cependant) ou encore *while* (tandis que).
- Pour indiquer une ..., on peut utiliser *too* (aussi), *similarly to* ou encore *in the same way as* (de la même façon).

→ FLAP: Linking Words

Play with Words and Culture n° 4

Challenge 2 WORDS AND SENTENCES Relative Pronouns *who* and *which*

1 Take up the challenge!

Repérez les pronoms relatifs et **indiquez** les 2 énoncés qui composent chacune des phrases suivantes :

a. The election which took place in 1994 in South Africa was the first democratic one.

b. Nelson Mandela, who was the first black president, is still the symbol of freedom in South Africa.

À quoi correspondent ces pronoms relatifs ?

2 Find the rule!

Lorsque deux phrases sont reliées pour former un seul énoncé, on utilise le pronom relatif :

- ... pour une personne ;
- ... pour un objet ou un concept.

RECAP > p. 125
Play with Words and Sentences n° 10

Challenge 3 WORDS AND SOUNDS Words Ending with *-ism*

1 Take up the challenge!

Retrouvez dans la vidéo les mots anglais pour dire *colonialisme*, *racisme* et *sexisme*.

Que remarquez-vous ?

39 **Écoutez**-les attentivement et **répétez**-les.

2 Find the sound!

Généralement, les mots en « -isme » en français perdent le ... final à l'écrit en anglais et se prononcent /zəm/.

Play with Words and Sounds n° 12

Irregular Session

40 **Retrouvez** les trois verbes irréguliers *know*, *fight* et *become* dans le rabat à la fin du livre. **Écoutez**-les, **répétez**-les et **mémorisez**-les. **Révisez** les six verbes appris précédemment.

Play with...

WORDS AND CULTURE

Play with

1 **Complete** the sentences with the correct words from the list.

bank - school - library - chemist's - cinema

a. A ... has a collection of books for people to read or borrow, usually without payment.

b. Children are educated and they study in a ... .

c. The ... is the shop where I can get medicines after visiting the doctor.

d. I like going to the ... where I can watch movies.

e. When I need some money to go shopping, I go to the ... .

2 **Find the right place.**

a. The local office of the police:

P _ _ _ C _   S _ _ _ _ _ N

b. A building used for the administration of local government:

T _ W _   H _ _ _

c. A place where stamps are sold and from where letters are sent:

_ _ _ T   _ FF _ _ _

d. An artificial area of water for swimming:

S _ _ _ _ I _ _   _ _ O _

e. An institution providing medical and surgical treatment:

H _ _ _ I _ _ L

3 **Which places from exercises 1 and 2 are closed for bank holidays?**

4 **HANGMAN GAME Choose** a linking word and **give** the number of letters it is composed of. Your partner tries to guess it by suggesting letters. He has to find the word before the diagram of the hangman is completed.

_ L _ O

~~F~~ ~~E~~ ~~T~~ ~~B~~ ~~P~~

5 Mount Rushmore National Memorial is located in the Black Hills of South Dakota. It was sculpted by Gutzon Borglum and his son, Lincoln Borglum. The rock carving depicts the faces of four U.S. Presidents. **Search** the Internet and **find** who they are.

WORDS AND SENTENCES

6 **Are these verbs regular or irregular?**

start	commemorate	begin
limit	wait	play
vote	know	watch
want	give	do
find	fight	win
celebrate	symbolise	learn
listen	look	cook
call	teach	help
guess	come	choose

7 **Complete the sentences in the past tense. You can find some help with the list of irregular verbs at the end of your book.**

a. St George ... (to be) a soldier who ... (to fight) against a dragon.

b. He ... (to save) the princess and ... (to enter) the legend.

c. The inhabitants of Silene ... (to offer) a human sacrifice every day.

d. They ... (to be) grateful to St George.

e. In 2019, aside from England, other countries ... (to celebrate) St George's Day including Canada, Croatia, Portugal, Cyprus, Greece, Georgia, Serbia, Bulgaria, Romania, Bosnia and Herzegovina, and the Republic of Macedonia.

f. The English playwright William Shakespeare also ... (to die) on the 23rd of April.

8 ***In* or *on*? Match these dates with the right preposition.**

fourth of July - May - July 14th 1789 - 2022 - April 1994 - 1994 - 25-12

9 **Complete the sentences with the right date.**

the 23rd of April - 1789 - February - 2008 - July 14th - 14 February

a. Lovers usually give presents on ... .

b. The French Revolution and the election of Washington took place in ... .

c. People celebrate St George's Day on ... .

d. Roses are sold mainly in ... because of Valentine's Day.

e. Barack Obama, the first African-American president, was elected in ... .

f. In French cities, there are many fireworks on ... .

10 **Complete with *who* or *which*.**

a. The people ... first came to the USA were British.

b. Great Britain, ... is composed of England, Wales and Scotland, is part of the United Kingdom along with Northern Ireland.

c. The national day, ... is often a public holiday, is the symbol of nationhood in a country.

d. American people, ... are generally patriots, enjoy celebrating their national day on the 4th of July.

WORDS AND SOUNDS

11 **a. Classify these verbs depending on the right pronunciation of *-ed*.**

remembered - added - organised - finished - liked - wanted - travelled - wished - visited - decided

"/d/" "/t/" "/id/"

b. Read them and record them reading.

c. Listen to your classmate's recording and correct if necessary.

12 41 **a. Listen and repeat these words.**

colonialism - professionalism - terrorism - multiracialism - optimism - individualism - triumphalism - patriotism - tourism - civism

b. Clap your hands to find the number of syllables.

4 syllables

3 syllables

5 syllables

6 syllables

2 syllables

MISSION CONTROL

Vers B1

SCENARIO The language assistant of your school presents the celebration of the national day in her country.

MISSION CO / EOC / Médiation Listen to the language assistant's presentation, present the national day in your own country and explain the similarities and differences between the two celebrations.

1. **Faites des recherches sur Internet** et **notez** les éléments relatifs à la fête nationale de votre pays : nom, date, origine, symboles, drapeau, jour férié ou ouvré, festivités, etc.

2. 42 **Écoutez** la présentation de l'assistante de langue et **créez** la carte d'identité de la fête nationale qu'elle présente.
3. **Notez** les différences et les points communs entre les deux fêtes.
4. **Présentez** votre fête nationale et **comparez**-la avec celle du pays dont l'assistante est originaire.

KEY QUESTION How does the national day reflect the culture of a country? What do you think now?

Assess Yourself

	☺	😐	☹
Compétences de communication			
→ Comprendre la présentation d'un évènement historique, d'une tradition, d'une fête.			
→ Présenter les éléments clés des fêtes nationales.			
→ Comparer des fêtes traditionnelles.			
Compétences linguistiques			
→ Comprendre et utiliser le lexique lié à la thématique des fêtes nationales.			
→ Conjuguer les verbes au prétérit.			
→ Lire les dates et les introduire avec la préposition qui convient.			
→ Prononcer correctement les terminaisons *-ed* et *-ism*.			
Compétences transversales			
→ Écouter autrui et prendre des notes.			
→ Organiser ma présentation avec des mots de liaison (contraste et similitude, notamment).			
→ Parler clairement et distinctement.			

Micro Project

- Interdisciplinarité : parcours éducation artistique et culturelle – géographie

ESCAPE GAME: CANADA DAY

On your way to Canada to celebrate the national day, you are locked in a room at the airport. Find the code and unlock the door to escape.

JEU
Escape Game
www.lienmini.fr/40241-25

1 Let's Get Started!

1. **Go** online to the escape game.
2. **Watch** the trailer. You have 50 minutes to **complete** the mission before your plane takes off! Good luck!

2 Your Road Map

Discover clues and solve puzzles about Canada.

➤ Identify the symbols of Canada

1. **Watch** the video. **Play** the memory game and the crossword puzzle to **find** one number of the digit code.

➤ Locate the cities of Canada

2. **Locate** 6 main cities on the map of Canada to **find** another number of the digit code.

➤ Discover Canada Day

3. **Watch** the video and **answer** the questions: when? where? who? what? why? how? Then, **find** a new number of the digit code.

➤ Check your knowledge

4. **Answer** the quiz and **complete** the summary. Then, **find** one more number of the digit code.

➤ Arrange the numbers and find the code to unlock the door

3 Screenshot Challenge

After unlocking the door, **take** a screenshot of your final time to compare with your classmates.

The first one to unlock the door will be the winner!

Accompagner • Personnaliser

Présenter un travail ou un projet à l'oral

1. Observer

Method & Strategies
Tip 4 : S'exprimer à l'oral
FLAP: Pronunciation

1. **Prenez connaissance** de la carte mentale et du plan préparés par Robin pour sa présentation de projet autour de la journée de l'Europe. **Observez** sa méthode de travail.

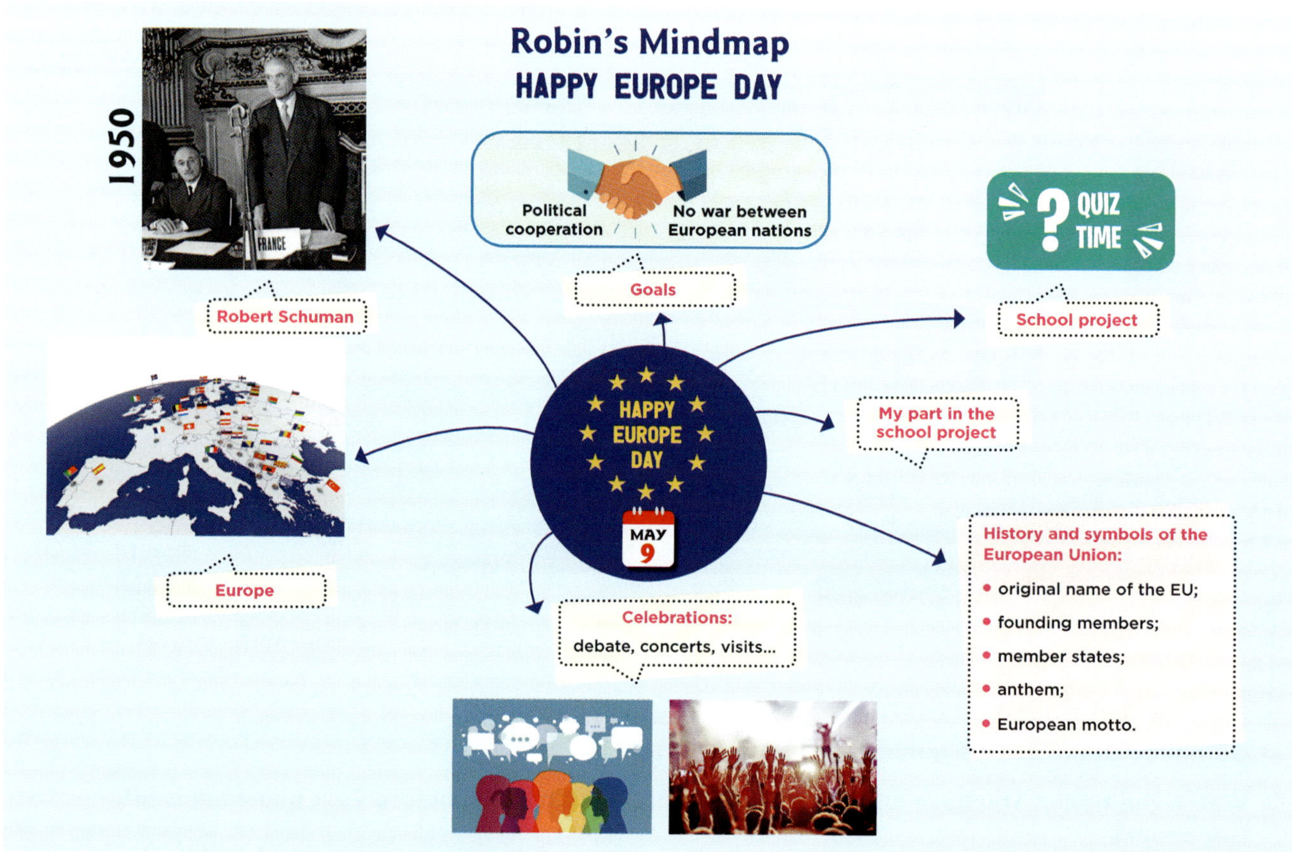

2. 43 **Écoutez** la présentation de Robin.

2. Identifier les stratégies

En vous aidant de la fiche **Method & Strategies n° 4** et des supports élaborés par Robin, **retrouvez** et **identifiez** les étapes et les stratégies mises en œuvre.

1. **Repérez** les différentes parties de la présentation.
2. **Repérez** les expressions proposées dans la fiche **Useful words and sentences** (p. 123) et utilisées par Robin dans sa présentation finale.

3. Appliquer

1. **Choisissez** un travail ou un court projet que vous avez préparé au cours de l'année.
2. **Appuyez-vous** sur la fiche **Method & Strategies n° 4** et **inspirez-vous** du plan et de la carte mentale de Robin.
3. **Présentez** votre travail ou votre projet.

Accompagner ● Ouvrir, Orienter, Oser

Oser partir à l'étranger

1. Comprendre comment me déplacer à Londres

1. **Regardez** la vidéo.
2. **Repérez** les conseils (*dos and don'ts*) donnés par le présentateur pour se déplacer dans le métro londonien.
3. **Listez** les monuments londoniens que vous connaissez. **Recherchez** ensuite sur Internet une carte touristique de Londres et **complétez** votre liste.

VIDEO
How to Use the London Underground / 1'28
www.lienmini.fr/40241-26

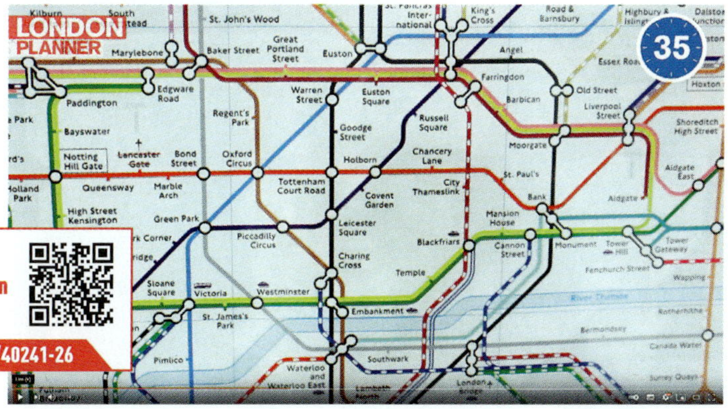

2. Préparer ma mobilité

Parcourez l'article « *Erasmus Bucket list* » et **identifiez** les 12 « choses à faire » pour profiter pleinement d'une mobilité à l'étranger.

ARTICLE
Erasmus Bucket list
www.lienmini.fr/40241-42

3. Oser

Vous avez trouvé un job d'été à Maidstone, dans le Kent britannique, et souhaitez en profiter pour découvrir Londres. Vous avez réservé un hébergement dans une auberge de jeunesse se trouvant près de Hyde Park.

1. **Créez** votre propre « *bucket list* » : **listez** au minimum 5 expériences différentes que vous souhaitez vivre pendant votre été.
2. **Faites** la liste des 5 lieux que vous souhaitez visiter à Londres.
3. **Prévoyez** vos itinéraires en métro : **cherchez** une carte de métro sur Internet, **trouvez** les lignes que vous utiliserez et les directions à prendre.

UNIT 6 Finding

Vers B1

- Grandes villes et habitat
- Modes et réseaux de transport

Look at the picture and describe what you see. What do you think about this city?

YOUR ROAD MAP

www.lienmini.fr/40241-27

UP TO YOU!

Easy Road
Extra Road
Bonus Road

KEY QUESTION How can we make the city a happy and easy place for everyone?

SCENARIO You take part in the opening of the next session of the World Urban Forum, organised by the United Nations. It will show different projects imagined by students from all over the world.

TASK 1 LIST-MAKING **EE** Create a collaborative list of important daily life characteristics.

TASK 2 PRESENTATION VIDEO **EOC** Put an oral commentary on a video to present a place to live in.

MISSION **EOC** / **EE** / **EOI** Invent the perfect place to live in and present it.

the Happy City

Open up!

Watch and listen to the song.

1. **Use the following words to talk about the document.**

   a. by the world-famous band – to accompany their song – in April 2020 – this video clip was released – the Rolling Stones – entitled *Living in a Ghost Town*

   b. the strange atmosphere – it shows – in London and other cities – during the first Covid-19 lockdown

2. **Choose from the list below the places or things you can see in the video.**

   the London underground – the Eiffel Tower – Trafalgar Square – streets in Los Angeles – an empty train – lots of people – a homeless man – Piccadilly Circus station – Buckingham Palace – a harmonica player – Big Ben

3. **Listen again and put the following lyrics into the right order as you hear them.**

   a. "Life was so beautiful / Then we all got locked down"

   b. "I'm going nowhere, shut up all alone"

   c. "Please let this be over / Stuck in a world without end"

   d. "I'm a ghost / Living in a ghost town"

   e. "Just staring at my phone"

VIDEO
The Rolling Stones – Living in a Ghost Town / 4'00
www.lienmini.fr/40241-28

WHAT ABOUT YOU?

1. **Describe** the atmosphere of the video. Which words below do you think are the best to qualify it? Why?

   creepy – fun – spooky – strange – joyful – scary – eerie – romantic – creative – boring – lively – weird

2. **Think** about London and other big cities. **Imagine** another title to describe a more positive and pleasant view of one of these cities.

Get ready!

In-Class Activities

EXERCICES
Flashcards
www.lienmini.fr/40241-29

1. **Look at** the flashcards and **listen to** the words. **Repeat.**

2. (44) **Listen, read and remember.**

   empty streets – deserted streets – anonymous streets – empty trains – empty underground stations – carless roads – lonely adverts – bright lights – a ghost town – worldwide problems

By yourself!

Find a photo of a famous town during the lockdown. **Think** about the empty streets and **describe** the place. Was the place where you live like this during the Covid-19 lockdowns in 2020?

Use an online dictionary to help you.

The 20-Minute City

VIDEO
What is a 20 minute city neighbourhood / 0.49
www.lienmini.fr/40241-30

Method & Strategies
Tip 2 : Comprendre un support audio ou vidéo

1. **Look at** a map and **find** where the city of Melbourne is (country, state, east / west / north / south...).
2. **Look at** the picture above. **Guess** what this video is about.
3. **Listen to** the video *with your eyes closed!* **Pay attention to** the numbers and all the words you know. **Find out** as much information as possible about the Melbourne plan. **Share** with your neighbour.
4. **Pay attention** to the words *livability* and *neighbourhood* at the beginning of the video.
   a. **Give** the words you see in them.
   b. **Guess** their meaning.
5. **Watch the video** again and **answer** the questions.
   a. What is the aim of the *Plan Melbourne* project?
   b. What sort of things / facilities should people have access to?

Extra Road Vers le Bac

6. The speaker says: "We are already working with..." According to you, which message does he want to pass on?

WHAT ABOUT YOU?

In groups, **complete** the list of buildings and public facilities you can find in a typical town. Does your town/ school's town have these facilities, too?

"What is a city, but the people; true the people are the city."
William Shakespeare (Coriolanus)

TASK 1

LIST-MAKING EE Create a collaborative list of important daily life characteristics.

1. **Make** a list of 5 features in a city that are important in your daily life.
2. **Compare** it with your partners': **explain** your choices, **agree** together on a collaborative list and **write** it down on a pad or a poster.

Help: See Annex p. 113.

Challenge yourself!

My Language Challenges	J'ai des difficultés ou je réponds non...
1. Je connais des adjectifs et des verbes pour qualifier des espaces de vie.	je fais le challenge n° 1.
2. Je comprends et sais exprimer le but ou l'objectif.	je fais le challenge n° 2.
3. Je sais prononcer les mots contenant la lettre « *i* ».	je fais le challenge n° 3.
4. Je sais construire et prononcer des adjectifs composés du suffixe *-able*.	je fais le challenge n° 4.

Challenge 4

Challenge 1 WORDS AND CULTURE City Life

1 Take up the challenge!

- **Repérez** dans la liste les adjectifs et les verbes employés dans la vidéo pour qualifier les espaces de vie.
  access – close – committed – convenient – cooperate – create – diverse – far – find out – get worse – improve – livable – local – make better – safe – similar – simplify – uncommitted – user-friendly – unlivable – unsafe – walkable – worldwide
- **Classez**-les (verbes ou adjectifs).

2 Find the word!

- **Associez** les adjectifs à leur contraire quand c'est possible.

Le contraire de l'adjectif :

- *close* est ... ;
- *committed* est ... ;
- *diverse* est ... ;
- *livable* est ... ;
- *local* est ... ;
- *safe* est ... .

Play with Words and Culture n° 1 à 6

Challenge 2 WORDS AND SENTENCES Goals

1 Take up the challenge!

Observez :

To improve livability, the Victorian Government is working...

Repérez l'expression que le présentateur utilise pour exprimer le but (pour, afin de). Quelle question pourrait-on poser pour obtenir cette réponse ?

2 Find the rule!

On utilise ... ou *in order to* pour exprimer le but en anglais.

Pour poser une question sur le but, on peut dire « *What is the ... ?* » ou encore « *What is the ... ?* ».

Attention : contrairement au français, on ne peut jamais utiliser *for* pour exprimer le but.

RECAP > p. 126
Play with Words and Sentences n° 8

Challenge 3 WORDS AND SOUNDS The Letter "i"

1 Take up the challenge!

45 **Écoutez** ces mots extraits de la vidéo.

a. livability b. communities
c. diverse d. facilities
e. industries f. find

La lettre « i » se prononce-t-elle toujours de la même façon ?

2 Find the sound!

La lettre « i » en anglais est souvent une source de confusion. Elle peut se prononcer :

- /aɪ/ comme dans ... ou ... ;
- /i/ comme dans ..., ... ou ... .

Remarque : l'ajout d'un « e » final change la prononciation de la lettre « i » : kit /i/ *vs* kite /aɪ/ ; trip /i/ *vs* tripe /aɪ/.

RECAP > p. 127
Play with Words and Sounds n° 10 et 11

Irregular Session

46 **Retrouvez** les trois verbes irréguliers ***build***, ***drink*** et ***go*** dans le rabat à la fin du livre. **Écoutez**-les, **répétez**-les et **mémorisez**-les.

2. READING ROAD

Vers B1

Open your Mind!

Floating Cities: Fantasy or the Future?

Floating cities have always seemed like a utopian pipe dream based on fantasy. Although it sounds like science fiction, the United Nations wants to make it a reality. As climate change advances at an alarming rate and huge numbers of people cram into city slums, "floating cities will be one of the possible solutions", UN-Habitat's executive director, Maimunah Mohd Sharif, says.

How will it work? Oceanix City, the name of the world's first sustainable floating city, will essentially be groups of hexagonal platforms – fixed to the seabed – that will each host about 300 residents, effectively creating a community for 10,000 residents. Marc Collins Chen, the CEO, said the technology won't be a problem as it already exists. "The biggest question in people's minds is if these cities actually float, will people live in them?" he wondered.

Are the plans realistic? "There are thousands of such houses in the Netherlands and other communities around the world. The challenge is now a question of scale because we will need to create integrated systems and new communities. "The main obstacles at this point are psychological and are not technological", said an observer.

People get psychologically nervous at the term "floating city". Yet, Oceanix makes its case for the ocean-based cities this way: "Close to 50 percent of people in the world live in coastal areas. The rising sea and climate change are compounding the problem. We believe humanity can live in harmony with life below water". We'll see how it actually turns out.

Adapted from www.foxnews.com and and bbc.com, April 2019

TIPS
UN: United Nations

1 **Look at the picture.**
a. What do you think it is?
1. a fish farm **2.** a millionaire's holiday paradise **3.** a sea city **4.** a mine **5.** something else (give details)
b. **Share** your ideas with your classmates and **discuss** them: which ideas are the best?

2 **Look at the document and choose the right answer.**
a. The document is a sci-fi / a media article.
b. It was published last year / many years ago / in April 2019.

3 **Read the title. Is it more negative than positive? Justify.**

4 Read the text.
a. **Point to the expressions which refer to "dream" and "reality".**
b. **Quote elements to show Oceanix is not a crazy dream or a fantasy.**

5 Read the text again.
a. **Match the labels below.**

The number of people on one platform	*thousands*
The number of floating houses in the Netherlands	*300*
The total number of inhabitants on Oceanix	*10,000*

b. **Write a sentence for each element.**

→ **Method & Strategies**
Tip 3 : Comprendre un support écrit

WHAT ABOUT YOU?

Can you imagine living on Oceanix or in a similar sort of futuristic city? **Share** your ideas with your group. What do they think?

"We build the Perfect City time shall never alter."
W. H. Auden

Extra Road Vers le Bac

6 **Read the end of the article.**
a. **Find the main reason why the Oceanix project is a positive or necessary idea.**
b. **Find an important disadvantage to the project.**

TASK 2

PRESENTATION VIDEO EOC Put an oral commentary on a video to present a place to live in.

1 **Go** to the Oceanix website (media). **Choose** a video and **put** your commentary **on** it to promote living on the artificial island.

2 **Present** your video to the class.

Challenge yourself!

My Language Challenges	J'ai des difficultés ou je réponds non…
1. Je connais plusieurs noms, verbes et adjectifs pour parler du rêve et de la réalité.	je fais le challenge n° 1.
2. Je sais poser une question et m'exprimer sur une idée future.	je fais le challenge n° 2.
3. Je suis capable de prononcer des mots contenant des lettres muettes.	je fais le challenge n° 3.
4. Je suis capable d'identifier des sigles internationaux.	je fais le challenge n° 4.

Challenge 4

Challenge 1 WORDS AND CULTURE Dream and Reality

1 Take up the challenge!

Classez les mots suivants selon qu'ils se rapportent au champ lexical du rêve ou de la réalité.

utopian - fantasy - reality - to exist - possible - realistic - dream - pipe dream - myth - truth - imagination - fact - to come true - fantastic

2 Find the word!

47 **Écoutez** ces mots et **mémorisez** ce lexique. **Précisez** s'il s'agit de verbes (V), de noms (N) ou d'adjectifs (A).

Play with Words and Culture n° 7

Challenge 2 WORDS AND SENTENCES Future

1 Take up the challenge!

Observez :

a. Floating cities will be one of the possible solutions.

b. How will it work?

c. We'll see how it actually turns out.

- **Quel est l'auxiliaire utilisé dans chacune de ces phrases ? De quel temps s'agit-il ?**
- **À quoi correspond « *'ll* » ?**

2 Find the rule!

Pour exprimer une action …, on ajoute l'auxiliaire … (forme contractée : …) devant la base verbale.

- **À la forme interrogative, on inverse l'auxiliaire et le sujet.**
- **À la forme négative, on ajoute « *not* » entre l'auxiliaire et le verbe (forme contractée : *won't*).**

Exemple : When will it become true? It will become true within 30 years. It won't be long.

RECAP > p. 126
Play with Words and Sentences n° 9

Challenge 3 WORDS AND SOUNDS Silent Letters

1 Take up the challenge!

48 **Écoutez** ces mots.

would - could - listen - psychological

Comparez leur prononciation avec leur écriture : toutes les lettres sont-elles prononcées ?

2 Find the sound!

En anglais, certaines consonnes sont ….

- **La lettre … dans *climb, doubt, bomb, debt*.**
- **La lettre … dans *know, knock, knife, knee*.**
- **La lettre … dans *answer, two, sword, wrap*.**
- **La lettre … dans *mechanic, hour, school, what*.**

RECAP > p. 127
Play with Words and Sounds n° 12

Irregular Session

49 **Retrouvez** les trois verbes irréguliers ***fly***, ***forget*** et ***dream*** dans le rabat à la fin du livre. **Écoutez**-les, **répétez**-les et **mémorisez**-les. **Révisez** les trois verbes appris précédemment.

Play with...

WORDS AND CULTURE

1 **Match** the English words with their French equivalents.

a. eerie - safe - livable - close - spooky - committed - sustainable - obvious - smart

b. durable - engagé - évident - inquiétant - intelligent - proche - sûr - troublant - vivable

2 **Match** some of the words from exercise 1 with the right definitions.

a. Something which is not dangerous.

b. It can continue for a long time because it does not hurt the environment.

c. Something which is near in terms of distance or of time.

d. It is completely clear and everyone knows it.

e. This is really clever or intelligent.

f. For a place, it is quite good or acceptable but not fantastic.

3 **Find** words from exercise 1 which go well in the sentences below.

a. Everyone dreams of a home which is maybe not perfect but ... and ... .

b. People do not like to live far from work but prefer it if it is ... .

c. We think it is important to be ... to the idea of making the world a better place.

d. It is ... that we need ... cities to make life easier.

4 Lagos, London or Melbourne? **Match** each city with the right information. **Search** the Internet if necessary.

a. ... is in Australia in Oceania.

b. ... is in Nigeria in Africa.

c. ... is in the United Kingdom in Europe.

d. ... is famous for its financial centre and has 9.7 million inhabitants.

e. ... has 5 million people and it is said to be the most livable city in the world.

f. ... is famous for Afrobeat music and has over 20 million inhabitants.

5 Lagos, London or Melbourne? **Look** at the pictures and **decide** which city it is. **Search** the Internet when necessary.

a.

b.

c.

6 Lagos, London or Melbourne? **Read** the sentences to your partner and **get** him/her to guess which city it is.

a. This city is the largest city in its continent.

b. This city has about 9 football teams and 3 of them have always been in its Premier League. (Arsenal, Chelsea, Tottenham Hotspurs).

c. This city became the largest city in the country in 1851 when gold was found there.

d. Many people say this city is the best city in the world to live in.

e. This city is the home to Nollywood, the second-biggest cinema industry in the world.

f. In the centre of this city, a square metre of land cost an average of €25,000 in 2014.

7 **Give** synonyms to the words in colour in the sentences below.

a. Living on a floating city is not a **utopian dream** but is an idea that could become **fact** one day.

b. It is definitely not **crazy imagination** but an idea that will probably **exist** one day.

c. It is really an **incredible** idea.

WORDS AND SENTENCES

8 The sentences below have got mixed up. Can you put them back together again?

To make a city user-friendly and convenient

everything should be only 20 minutes from where we live.

To build floating cities in the sea

everyone needs to feel comfortable living there.

To make cities really inclusive and open

we will need to build floating cities.

To feel safe when we live near the sea

people won't need cars.

To move around the floating city

we need really good engineers.

9 **Let's dream** about the ideal future. **Complete** these predictions with the right form of *will* and the verbs into brackets.

a. Every house ... equipped with solar panels to generate electricity. (be)

b. People ... electric cars. (drive)

c. Factories ... the air. (pollute)

d. I'm afraid people ... and live on floating cities. (come)

e. Our future ... greener and more sustainable. (be)

WORDS AND SOUNDS

10 a. **Challenge** your friends with these very famous tongue twisters. **Time** yourself and see how many words you can say before you get stuck.

1. Peter Piper picked a peck of pickled peppers.

2. A peck of pickled peppers Peter Piper picked.

3. If Peter Piper picked a peck of pickled peppers.

4. Where's the peck of pickled peppers Peter Piper picked?

b. 50 **Listen to** the tongue twisters to check your pronunciation.

11 **Read** the words and **classify** them depending on the pronunciation of the letters "i" and "y".

describe – city – life – my – lively – anonymous – cycle – 20 minutes – listen – facility – worldwide – improve – sci-fi – realistic – myth – climb – psychology – million

"/aɪ/ like in "I" or "cry""

"/ɪ/ like in "big" or "sit""

12 Read the following sentences aloud but don't pronounce the silent letters!

a. "I know it's Wednesday," she said romantically!

b. "I doubt it's a sword but a knife," he said logically.

c. This island is so calm, my friend.

MISSION CONTROL

Vers B1

SCENARIO You take part in the opening of the next session of the World Urban Forum, organised by the United Nations. It will show different projects imagined by students from all over the world.

MISSION EOC / EE / EOI Invent the perfect place to live in and present it.

1. En groupe, **choisissez** les éléments qui composeront le lieu dans lequel les gens seront heureux :
   - Où se situera-t-il (montagne, mer, espace, etc.) ?
   - Quels bâtiments, espaces de vie contiendra-t-il ?
   - Comment les gens se déplaceront-ils (transports, etc.) ?
   - Quelles seront les règles pour que les habitants fassent bon usage de ce lieu parfait ?
   - Quels seront les objectifs de votre projet ?
2. **Imaginez** ensemble le dessin, le plan ou la carte de votre ville idéale ou de votre lieu de vie idéal.
3. **Répartissez-vous** les tâches :
   - **Présentez** à l'écrit votre lieu de vie idéal en expliquant vos choix dans 1 paragraphe de 100 mots minimum. **Complétez** votre présentation avec votre carte, dessin ou plan ;
   - **Présentez** oralement votre projet en 3 minutes minimum. **Affichez** ou **projetez** votre illustration finale, **décrivez** votre lieu idéal et **expliquez** vos choix. **Répondez** également aux commentaires et questions de vos camarades.

   N'oubliez pas d'utiliser des mots de liaison, le vocabulaire de l'unité autour du rêve et de la réalité, ainsi que le futur.
4. **Écoutez** la présentation des projets de vos camarades et **prenez des notes** en indiquant dans deux colonnes distinctes ce qui vous plait et déplait dans ces projets.
5. **Préparez** des questions à poser à vos camarades à propos de leur projet.
6. **Choisissez** le projet qui vous plait le plus et **justifiez** votre opinion.
   Votez pour le projet qui représentera votre école au Forum urbain mondial des Nations Unies.

KEY QUESTION How can we make the city a happy and easy place for everyone?
What do you think now?

Assess Yourself

	🙂	😐	☹️
Compétences de communication			
→ Présenter un projet futur.			
→ Décrire et qualifier des espaces de vie.			
→ Donner mon avis sur un projet.			
Compétences linguistiques			
→ Utiliser le lexique approprié : villes, modes de vie, rêve et réalité ; le prononcer correctement.			
→ Utiliser le futur.			
→ Exprimer le but ou l'objectif.			
Compétences transversales			
→ Collaborer, être engagé et impliqué.			
→ Être créatif et faire des choix.			
→ Adopter un rythme de parole adéquat et être convaincant.			
→ Organiser mon écrit de façon cohérente.			

Exam Road

COMPRÉHENSION DE L'ÉCRIT

CO EE

The "Colour Palace" at the Dulwich Picture Gallery (art gallery opened in 1817), by Yinka Ilori and Pricegore architects, London, 2019.

Yinka Ilori and Colour in London: Happy Street and The Colour Palace with Pricegore

Metalocus, 31 July 2019.

"The Colour Palace" [...] located outside the Dulwich Picture Gallery [...] designed by Yinka Illori, is a fusion of West African and European influences. On the one hand, it is inspired by the colourful African textiles found hanging throughout the markets of Balogun in Lagos, Nigeria, and on the other hand, the symmetry, curves and right angles of Sir John Soane's iconic Dulwich Picture Gallery design.

The Colour Palace is a 10-metre-high cube with a bold geometric pattern, standing on four huge red cylinders. [...]

Illori's second project is another colourful installation called *Happy Street*, built with bright-patterned panels which envelop the Thessaly Road railway in South London.

"Happy Street" realm comprises 56 patterned-enamel panels decorated with 16 different colours. Bringing together the community, a primary school and use low-cost material and durability, the installation creates an inviting environment underneath the bridge, previously a "dark and dangerous urban context".

Both of Illori's projects focus on transforming the community and its surroundings by using color as a gateway for change, inclusion, and an inviting sense of community.

https://www.metalocus.es

Lisez le texte ci-dessus puis **faites-en** un compte-rendu écrit en français.

1. Vous **préciserez** : la nature et le thème principal du document ; les lieux décrits, leur localisation et leurs caractéristiques ; l'effet produit par chacun des lieux ; l'objectif de l'artiste.

2. Vous **conclurez** votre compte-rendu en expliquant la fonction du document. S'agit-il de relater, d'informer, de convaincre, de critiquer, de dénoncer ou de divertir ?

EXPRESSION ORALE EN CONTINU

Présentez et **rendez compte** en anglais du projet réalisé en cours d'anglais autour de la ville idéale. Pour **organiser** votre prise de parole (3 minutes minimum), vous pourrez indiquer :
- si vous aviez déjà réfléchi au sujet avant de l'étudier en classe ;
- ce que vous avez appris concernant le sujet ;
- quel était l'objectif du projet ;
- quelles étapes vous ont amené à réussir la mission ;
- quelle partie vous avez préférée / le moins appréciée dans ce projet ;
- quelles difficultés vous avez rencontrées et comment vous les avez surmontées ;
- ce que ce projet vous a apporté d'un point de vue personnel et professionnel.

Pensez à donner des exemples !

Rappel : l'attendu au baccalauréat sera de 5 minutes.

EXPRESSION ORALE EN INTERACTION

51

Écoutez les questions et **enregistrez** vos réponses.

a. **Repérez** le mot interrogatif utilisé dans la question.

b. **Appuyez-vous** sur les mots de la question pour répondre et soyez attentif à la prononciation.

c. **Justifiez** vos réponses par des exemples.

Accompagner • Personnaliser

M'exprimer à l'écrit

→ Method & Strategies
Tip 5 : S'exprimer à l'écrit

1. Observer

Sarah doit répondre à la consigne suivante :

"What I like about cities is that everything is king size, the beauty and the ugliness." Write a paragraph to explain what Joseph Brodsky means. Give examples and tell if you agree with him. (100 à 120 mots minimum, hors citation.)

1 **Prenez connaissance** des documents élaborés par Sarah pour répondre à la consigne et **observez** sa méthode de travail.

Document 1 : le sujet

Citation : "What I like about cities is that everything is king size, the beauty and the ugliness."

→ **le contexte** : social life
→ **les mots-clés** : cities, beauty, ugliness, size
→ *everything* : tout
→ **le temps** : présent simple
→ *king size* : size = la taille ; king = le roi → de grande taille
→ *I like* : What the author thinks, positive opinion

Auteur : Joseph Brodsky → a Russian-American author, a contemporary poet

Consigne : Write a paragraph to explain what Joseph Brodsky means. Give examples and tell if you agree with him. (100 à 120 mots minimum, hors citation)

→ **Verbes** : to write, to explain, to give (examples), to tell (my opinion)

Document 2 : mes idées et mon plan

Introduction :

→ **ma phrase introductive** : Joseph Brodsky says: (quotation)
→ **mon plan** : 1st **part** (to explain, to give examples) ; 2nd **part**: to give my opinion...

1re partie : expliquer et donner des exemples

Very large streets or avenues (Fifth Avenue); very big parks (Central Park); very high skyscrapers (the Empire State building); very large statues (the 350-foot-high Statue of Liberty).

THE CITY

- Example – New York
- Beauty / Ugliness – Elegant, beautiful, inelegant, ugly...
- King size – Streets, avenues, parks, skyscrapers, statues, monuments, noise, pollution, traffic, poverty / big, extreme, large, high, impressive...
- What I like about cities – Monuments, architecture, skyline, shops, leisure facilities (museums, theatres, cinemas...) / lively, pleasant, attractive...
- What I dislike about cities – Overcrowded streets, noise, dirty, polluted, unsafe, uniform...

2e partie: donner mon avis

+ visiting famous buildings, watching the skyline of very big cities.

- the noise of big cities, unsafe, uniform, dirty, overcrowded.

Conclusion: Visiting big cities is wonderful / I prefer small towns

Document 3 : mon premier jet d'écriture

Introduction

Joseph Brodsky, a Russian-American author, says: "...".

I will explain what the author means and give examples to illustrate it. I will give my opinion about what he says.

1st part

The author has a positive opinion about cities: everything is big in towns. They may be beautiful or ugly.

This elegance or ugliness is always extreme: he appreciates this contrast.

In New York, there are very large streets or avenues (Fifth Avenue), very big parks (Central Park), very high skyscrapers (the Empire State building), very impressive statues (the Statue of Liberty/350 feet tall).

Noise, traffic and pollution are very important problems.

2nd part

I agree with Joseph Brodsky: I love the skyline, monuments, shops, leisure facilities...

I dislike the noise of big cities. Cities are unsafe, uniform, dirty, overcrowded.

Conclusion: Visiting big cities is a wonderful experience. I prefer living in a small town.

2 **Lisez sa production finale.**

Document 4 : ma production finale

Joseph Brodsky, a Russian-American author, says: " What I like about cities is that everything is king size, the beauty and the ugliness".

First, I will explain what the author means and give examples to illustrate it. Then, I will give my opinion about what he says.

To begin with, the author has a positive opinion about cities. He means that everything is big in towns. They may be beautiful or ugly. But this elegance or ugliness is always extreme and he appreciates this contrast. On the contrary to villages or small towns, nothing is small: in New York, for example, there are very large streets or avenues, like Fifth Avenue; very big parks, like Central Park, and very high skyscrapers, like the Empire State building. You can ever see giant statues. For example, the Statue of Liberty is 305 feet high. It's really impressive! But noise, traffic, pollution and poverty are very important problems too.

On the one hand, I agree with Joseph Brodsky because I enjoy visiting famous monuments and I love the architecture and the skyline of very big cities. They are very attractive. The number of shops and leisure facilities is very important as well. There are lots of cinemas, museums and theatres. It is lively and pleasant. Everything is at walking distance. On the other hand, I think that cities are sometimes unsafe, uniform and dirty. To my mind, streets are often overcrowded. Moreover, I dislike the noise of big cities.

To conclude, I would say that visiting big cities is a wonderful experience because everything is gigantic, but I prefer living in a small town.

2. Identifier les stratégies

En vous aidant de la fiche Method & Strategies n° 5 et des supports élaborés par Sarah, retrouvez et identifiez les étapes et les stratégies qu'elle a mises en œuvre.

1. Premier document, **repérez** la stratégie choisie pour identifier la thématique et comprendre ce qui est attendu.
2. Document 2, **repérez** la forme retenue par Sarah pour noter ses idées, pour les organiser.
3. Document 3, **identifiez** les éléments ajoutés par Sarah pour passer de la prise de notes à la rédaction d'énoncés. **Repérez** la structuration du propos et le temps majoritairement utilisé.
4. Document 4, **repérez** les verbes introducteurs (il dit que, je pense que...) et les mots de liaison ajoutés. Qu'expriment-ils ?

3. Appliquer

1 **Lisez la consigne suivante :**

> *"The city is not all bad nor all good. It is humanity compressed." Lyman Abbott*
> *Write a paragraph to explain what Lyman Abbott means. Give examples and tell if you agree with him.*

2 **Inspirez-vous** de la fiche **Method & Strategies n° 5** et du travail de Sarah pour commenter la citation.

3 **Écrivez** un paragraphe de 80 à 100 mots minimum pour répondre à la consigne.

UNIT 7 Take a Walk

Vers B1

- Les grandes problématiques d'actualité et leurs incidences
- Engagement humanitaire et citoyen

Look at the picture and **give** as many words as possible to **describe** it. **Guess** what it is about.

YOUR ROAD MAP

www.lienmini.fr/40241-31

UP TO YOU!

- Easy Road
- Extra Road
- Bonus Road

KEY QUESTION How can we bring humans and nature together?

SCENARIO Your vocational school organises a multilingual video contest called *#WeNeedAction* to support Earth Day on April 22nd.

TASK 1 CATCHY SLOGAN **EE** Write a slogan urging people to make a move.

TASK 2 EASY ECO-TIPS **EOI** Talk about eco-tips to encourage your friend to become eco-friendly.

TASK 3 GREEN COMPANIES **EOC** Present a company which fights for a green cause.

MISSION **EOC** Create a one-minute video to celebrate Earth Day at school, promote environmental awareness and encourage your schoolmates to take action for nature.

on the Green Side!

Open up!

VIDEO
Le moment est venu de donner la priorité à la nature / 1'19
www.lienmini.fr/40241-32

1. **Watch** the video. Which emotion does it convey? **Listen to** the speaker's voice and to the music.
2. **Watch** the video **again** and **say** what is in danger. **Give** precise examples.
3. **Last viewing.** What is the main message delivered by António Guterres, the United Nations Secretary-General? What event does he promote? **Identify** the goal of this event.

WHAT ABOUT YOU?

1. For you, what are the biggest environmental issues?
2. Do you feel involved in these issues? **Explain** why.

Get ready!

In-Class Activities

EXERCICES
flashcards
www.lienmini.fr/40241-33

1. a. **Look at** the flashcards and **listen to** the words.
   b. **Repeat.**
   c. **Memorise** the way the words are written.
2. **Try** and **remember** as many words as you can. **Share** with your partner.

a

b

c

d

e

f

By yourself!

Match these English words with their French equivalents.

1. reduce **2.** reuse
3. recycle **4.** eco-friendly
5. sustainable **6.** waste

a. respectueux de l'environnement
b. diminuer
c. des déchets
d. réutiliser
e. recycler
f. renouvelable, durable

Raise your Voice!

VIDEO
'Less Meat Less Heat' starring Gov. Arnold Schwarzenegger / 0'45
www.lienmini.fr/40241-34

→ **Method & Strategies**
Tip 2 : Comprendre un support audio ou vidéo

1. **Watch** and **listen to** the video.
   a. **Give** as much information as you can about the character (name, nationality, physical description, job...).
   b. Which environmental organisation is at the origin of this video?
2. a. **Watch** the video **again** and **write down** all the words you know.
   b. What does the actor encourage people to do? **Share** with your partner.
3. a. **Match** the words you have heard with one of these categories.

   Problem | Fields in which we must make changes | The consequences of meat production

   b. **Listen again** and **complete** your work. What do we need to change to avoid catastrophic climate change?
4. **Watch again** and **answer** the questions.
   a. What are the consequences of high meat consumption?
   b. **Quote** the slogan of the video.

Extra Road Vers le Bac

5. Why was this actor chosen by the environmental organisation Wildaid?
6. Can you **guess** why the campaign is called "5 to do today"?

WHAT ABOUT YOU?

Give examples of food or drinks you could avoid to protect both your health and the planet.

"The earth is a fine place and worth fighting for."
Ernest Hemingway

TASK 1

CATCHY SLOGAN EE Write a slogan urging people to make a move.

1. **Get** into groups of 3 students. **Choose** a cause that matters to you (water pollution, forest conservation, recycling...) and **prepare** a list of words related to it.
2. **Brainstorm** to create a catchy slogan encouraging eco-awareness and actions to protect the environment.

Help: A good slogan is short, uses rhymes, the imperative form and plays on words.
Examples: Get the Hint, Don't Leave Your Footprint! / Be mature, save nature! / Wait, Stop and Think. Save Water to Drink!

Challenge yourself!

My Language Challenges	J'ai des difficultés ou je réponds non...
1. Je connais le vocabulaire du dérèglement climatique.	je fais le challenge n° 1.
2. Je suis capable d'utiliser l'impératif pour faire une recommandation (forme affirmative et négative).	je fais le challenge n° 2.
3. Je sais distinguer les sons /i/ et /i:/.	je fais le challenge n° 3.
4. Je sais comment exprimer la nécessité avec *need to*.	je fais le challenge n° 4.

Challenge 4

Challenge 1 WORDS AND CULTURE Climate Disruption

1 Take up the challenge!

Sélectionnez dans cette liste tous les mots prononcés ou représentés dans la vidéo :

storm – flood – climate change – acid rain – fire – global warming – drought – greenhouse gas

2 Find the word!

52 **Vérifiez** vos réponses et **mémorisez**-les.

Play with Words and Culture n° 1

Challenge 2 WORDS AND SENTENCES Recommendations

1 Take up the challenge!

Observez :

a. Please consider eating less meat!

b. Please, don't eat too much meat!

- **Observez** la ponctuation, **repérez** le verbe et **indiquez** le mode et la forme utilisés. Qu'expriment-ils ?
- Que constatez-vous à la forme négative ?

2 Find the rule!

Pour recommander ou suggérer fortement, on utilise ... .

À la forme affirmative : ... .

À la forme négative : ... + base verbale !

RECAP > p. 126
Play with Words and Sentences n° 4

Challenge 3 WORDS AND SOUNDS /i/ *vs* /i:/

1 Take up the challenge!

53 **Écoutez et répétez** les mots suivants entendus dans la vidéo.

meat – *heat* – *issue* – *need* – *consider* – *please*

- Quel est leur point commun ?
- Quelle différence remarquez-vous entre les mots en couleur et ceux qui ne le sont pas?

2 Find the rule!

Le son « i » peut être ... /i/ ou /i:/.

Le son /i:/ peut ... de différentes façons :

- « ea » comme dans *meat* ;
- « ee » comme dans *need* ;
- « ie » comme dans *field* ;
- « ei » comme dans *ceiling* ;
- « eo » comme dans *people* ;
- « i » comme dans *machine*.

RECAP > p. 127
Play with Words and Sounds n° 10

Irregular Session

54 **Retrouvez** les trois verbes irréguliers *eat*, *lead* et *leave* dans le rabat à la fin du livre. **Écoutez**-les, **répétez**-les et **mémorisez**-les.

Green up!

Students Can Go Green

Elizabeth Hoyt – August 17, 2019

Believe it or not, you can be kind to the planet [...] without much effort at all. Here are easy ways you can live greener and reduce your carbon footprint* while you're a student.

1. **Take Notes Electronically:** Thankfully, the world is now digitally focused and your studies can be, too. You'll save money (and stop wasting paper) on purchasing notebooks [...] if you begin to electronically take down* what you need to remember in class.

2. **Adopt Reusable Bag Practices:** Take reusable bags instead of opting for paper or plastic. It's wasteful and unnecessary [...].

3. **Nix* Bottled Water:** Purchase water bottles that you can refill instead of tossing out a new bottle every time you need to quench your thirst*. It's estimated that up to 80 percent of water bottles in the United States never get recycled. [...]

4. **Recycle:** By now, this should be a no-brainer*. When you're able, recycle. Whether it's paper products, plastics or upcycling old items, it's important to think about which trash can be saved from a landfill.

5. **Power Down:** When you're not using appliances* or you're not in a room, turn off lights and other electronics. [...] Bonus: your electric bill will thank you!

6. **Buy Less or Borrow:** Only buy what you actually need. In a consumer culture, it's easy to fall into overbuying habits. If you have the option, borrow items instead of buying them.

www.fastweb.com

TIPS

appliance: un appareil
carbon footprint: l'empreinte carbone
It's a no-brainer: ça coule de source
to nix: rejeter, refuser
to quench one's thirst: étancher sa soif
to take down: prendre des notes

1. **Look at** all the information around the document and **present** it.
2. **Read the introduction: what is the journalist's goal?**

→ Method & Strategies
Tip 3 : Comprendre un support écrit

3. **Read the whole text and cross out the subjects which are not discussed in the document.**
   school – shopping – eating habits – energy – hobbies – means of transport – fashion – recycling
4. **Find in the document the contrary to:**
   a. mean b. with c. difficult d. spend money e. save paper
   f. destroyed in g. turn on h. more i. buy
5. **Read the text again and answer the questions.**
   a. What can students do at school to reduce their carbon footprint?
   b. What is the problem with water bottles in the USA? How could it be fixed?
   c. What are the tips addressed to shopping lovers?

WHAT ABOUT YOU?

What changes have you already made in your everyday life to protect the planet?

Extra Road Vers le Bac

6. Which materials can be recycled and should be saved from landfills?
7. **Explain** why eco-friendly students don't pay huge electric bills.

"Our planet's alarm is going off, and it is time to wake up and take action!"
Leonardo DiCaprio

TASK 2

EASY ECO-TIPS EOI Talk about eco-tips to encourage your friend to become eco-friendly.

1. **Think** about three things you do every day which harm the environment.
2. **Tell** your partner about them. He/she will give you eco-tips and **explain** what will happen if you quit those bad habits. **Swap** roles!

Example: I drive to school every day. → Carpool with friends or take the bus! If you do so, you will cut down on exhaust gas.

Challenge yourself!

My Language Challenges	J'ai des difficultés ou je réponds non...
1. Je connais au moins 4 verbes d'action écoresponsables.	je fais le challenge n° 1.
2. Je sais comment exprimer une condition.	je fais le challenge n° 2.
3. Je sais prononcer *want* et *won't* et les distinguer.	je fais le challenge n° 3.
4. Je sais expliquer ce qu'est le Earth Overshoot Day.	je fais le challenge n° 4.

Challenge 4

Challenge 1 WORDS AND CULTURE Green Attitudes

1 Take up the challenge!

Relevez dans le texte les verbes d'action écoresponsables associés aux éléments suivants :

a. water bottles **b.** old items
c. new items **d.** lights or electronics

Associez-les aux traductions suivantes :

couper / éteindre - surcycler - remplir à nouveau - emprunter

2 Find the word!

55 **Vérifiez** vos réponses et **mémorisez** ce vocabulaire.

Enrichissez votre lexique écocitoyen en cherchant dans un dictionnaire (papier ou en ligne) le sens des mots suivants :

save leftovers - buy local - carpool - compost waste - eat organic food

Play with Words and Culture n° 3

Challenge 2 WORDS AND SENTENCES Conditions

1 Take up the challenge!

Observez cette phrase :

You'll save money if you electronically take down notes.

- **Déterminez** les deux propositions qui composent cette phrase.
- **Indiquez** les temps employés.
- **Trouvez** la conjonction qui permet d'introduire la condition.

2 Find the rule!

Pour exprimer une condition, on utilise une subordonnée qui commence avec la conjonction ... .

Elle est suivie du sujet et du verbe au présent.

La principale est au ... (S + *will/won't* + BV).

Exemple : If you compost your kitchen waste, you will get fertiliser for free.

RECAP > p. 126
Play with Words and Sentences n° 7, 8 et 9

Challenge 3 WORDS AND SOUNDS *Want* or *Won't*?

1 Take up the challenge!

56 **Écoutez** attentivement ces deux phrases :

a. You **won't** notice any difference.
b. You **want** to notice the difference.

Indiquez s'il existe une différence de prononciation entre *won't* et *want*. Si oui, laquelle ?

2 Find the sound!

Sélectionnez l'élément correct :

- *Want* → /wɒnt/ → verbe « vouloir » : ☐ un seul son ☐ un double son voyelle (ou diphtongue).
- *Won't* → /wəʊnt/ → contraction de *will* + *not* : ☐ un seul son ☐ un double son voyelle (ou diphtongue).

RECAP > p. 127
Play with Words and Sounds n° 11

Irregular Session

57 **Retrouvez** les trois verbes irréguliers ***begin***, ***get*** et ***buy*** dans le rabat à la fin du livre. **Écoutez**-les, **répétez**-les et **mémorisez**-les. **Révisez** les trois verbes appris précédemment.

Change the Tide!

VIDEO
Our Mission / 1'58
www.lienmini.fr/40241-35

→ Method & Strategies
Tip 2 : Comprendre un support audio ou vidéo

Company ID Card

Business name	4Ocean
Headquarters location	Boca Raton, Florida, USA
Creation date	2017

1 **Watch** the whole video with the *sound off*.
a. **Note down** all the words you could use to describe what you see.
b. **Discuss** with your group what type of video you think it is.

2 **Turn** the *sound on*, **watch again. Use** the time code below and **stop** your viewing. Then **answer** the questions.
a. ISSUE **Stop at 0'23.** What issue does the video raise? **Give precise information.**
b. PROBLEMS **Stop at 0'49.** Why is plastic such a huge problem?
c. MISSION **Stop at 1'04.** What is 4Ocean's mission?
d. ACTIONS **Watch** the end of the video and **list** the different actions 4Ocean carries out.
e. SLOGAN **Write** down 4Ocean's slogan.

3 **CHAIN SPEAKING ACTIVITY Use** the information above to present 4Ocean and the cause it fights for. One of your classmates makes a first suggestion. **Repeat** it and **complete** with a second one. **Go on** up to the end.

WHAT ABOUT YOU?

1 Which plastic objects are you ready to get rid of? How would you replace them?

2 Would you like to volunteer for a good cause? Why? Why not?

Extra Road Vers le Bac

4 **Give** a precise description of the "Clean Ocean Club" logo and **explain** the choice of its symbols.

Only if we understand, can we care.
Only if we care, we will help.
Only if we help, we shall be saved.

Jane Goodall

TASK 3

GREEN COMPANIES EOC **Present** a company which fights for a green cause.
Speak about its mission, the problem it wants to solve, the actions it carries out and **quote** its slogan. **Don't forget to** use linking words.
Need ideas? Ecosia, WWF, Inglorious Fruit and Vegetables...

Challenge yourself!

My Language Challenges	J'ai des difficultés ou je réponds non...
1. Je connais au moins 6 adjectifs liés à l'écologie.	je fais le challenge n° 1.
2. Je suis capable d'exprimer l'absence d'obligation avec *don't have to*.	je fais le challenge n° 2.
3. Je sais prononcer la lettre « a ».	je fais le challenge n° 3.
4. Je maitrise quelques unités de mesure britanniques.	je fais le challenge n° 4.

Challenge 4

Challenge 1 WORDS AND CULTURE Green Vocabulary

1 Take up the challenge!

Parmi les adjectifs suivants, retrouvez les trois entendus dans la vidéo :

renewable – organic – dependent on – biodegradable – sustainable – single-use – reusable

2 Find the word!

Associez chaque adjectif à son équivalent français :

biologique – à usage unique – biodégradable – renouvelable – réutilisable – dépendant de – durable

58 **Écoutez et mémorisez** les paires obtenues.

Play with Words and Culture n° 2

Challenge 2 WORDS AND SENTENCES Don't Have to

1 Take up the challenge!

Observez :

a. We don't have to be so dependent on plastic.

b. We don't have to sacrifice the environment.

Relevez les groupes verbaux.

- Comment sont-ils construits ?
- Quelle notion est exprimée ?

2 Find the rule!

On utilise *don't/doesn't have to* pour exprimer ... .

→ S + *don't/doesn't have to* + BV

RECAP > p. 126
Play with Words and Sentences n° 6 et 9

Challenge 3 WORDS AND SOUNDS The Letter "a"

1 Take up the challenge!

a. **Repérez** les mots suivants dans la vidéo :

plastic – estimated – facing – shape – engaged – trash – habits – apart – started

- Que remarquez-vous concernant la prononciation de la lettre « a » ?

59 b. **Regardez, écoutez** et **répétez** les mots suivants :

waste – glass – bad

- **Associez** chacun de ces mots aux mots précédents en fonction de leur prononciation.

2 Find the sound!

La lettre « a » peut se prononcer de plusieurs façons :

- /ei/ comme dans *bacon* ;
- /æ/ comme dans *man* ;
- /e/ comme dans *many* ;
- /i/ comme dans *message* ;
- /ɑ:/ comme dans *car* ;
- /əe/ comme dans *care* ;
- /ɒ/ comme dans *watch* ;
- /ɔ:/ comme dans *talk*.
- /ə/ comme dans *arrival* ;

RECAP > p. 127
Play with Words and Sounds n° 12

Irregular Session

60 **Retrouvez** les trois verbes irréguliers ***break***, ***sell*** et ***make*** dans le rabat à la fin du livre.
Écoutez-les, **répétez**-les et **mémorisez**-les. **Révisez** les six verbes appris précédemment.

Play with...

WORDS AND CULTURE

1 Match the following words with the right definitions.

acid rain – climate change – drought – fire – flood – global warming – greenhouse gas – storm

a. A violent disturbance in the atmosphere that brings rain, wind and thunder.
b. Rain that contains harmful chemicals.
c. Heat, light and flames produced by burning.
d. A long period with little or no rain.
e. Higher air and sea temperatures.
f. An overflow of water onto land.
g. Global changes in temperature, wind patterns, rainfall...
h. A gas in the atmosphere that stops heat from escaping into space.

2 Fill in the blanks with the right adjectives. You can use them only once!

reusable – *organic* – *dependent on* – *biodegradable* – *sustainable* – *renewable* – *single-use*

a. I buy ... food at the local farmer's market.
b. This factory is investing a lot of money in ... energy to become totally green.
c. Stop using ... plastic cups! They are not ... !
d. This furniture is made of wood from ... sources.
e. Don't forget your ... bags when going shopping.
f. We were not always ... plastic. In the past, milk was sold in glass bottles.

3 Match each picture with the right word.

a. to refill b. to upcycle c. to set your thermostat lower d. to turn off e. to save money f. to carpool

1

2

3

4

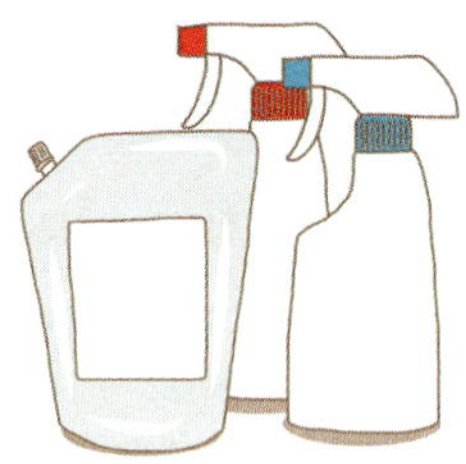
5

6

WORDS AND SENTENCES

4 **Complete the sentences with the right imperative form of the verbs (+ or –) to encourage ecofriendly attitudes.**

buy – recycle – turn off – drop – use – have

a. ... a bath. Have a shower instead!
b. ... bottled water! Prefer tap water!
c. ... public transports more often!
d. ... the lights when you leave a room!
e. ... used batteries!
f. ... litter in the nature!

5 **What is necessary to do in these situations? Imagine the end of the sentences.**

Example: I'm thirsty, I need to drink.

a. He is late, ...
b. You are sick, ...
c. She is tired, ...
d. My house is really dirty, ...

6 **Do you really have to do it? Complete these sentences with your classmates to explain what you do *not* have to do.**

Example: to have a lot of friends → You don't have to be a star to have a lot of friends.

a. ... to be happy.
b. ... to be strong and muscular.
c. ... to clean your bathroom. You can use white vinegar instead!
d. ... to quench your thirst. You can drink tap water.

7 **Use the right tense to complete the sentences.**

a. If we ... (not cut down) on waste rapidly, we ... (threaten) our own existence.
b. If he ... (recycle) his old items, there ... (be) less waste.
c. If they ... (not stop) cutting down trees, they ... (endanger) our oxygen supply.
d. If she ... (carpool) to the office, she ... (reduce) air pollution and traffic jams.

8 **Imagine what will change if you decide to...**

Example: make your own household cleaner → If I make my own household cleaner, I will save money.

a. compost your peelings.
b. collect rainwater.
c. line dry your clothes.
d. turn down junk mail.

9 a. **Look at** the picture and **name** as many waste as you can!
b. Then **explain** how you can stop creating those unnecessary trash.

WORDS AND SOUNDS

10 61 **Choose the word you hear.**

a. bin / bean
b. fill / feel
c. chick / cheek
d. sit / seat
e. will / wheel
f. grin / green

11 62 ***Want* or *won't*? Listen to the sentences and choose the word you hear.**

Won't	Want

12 a. **Match the words with the right sound.**

bath – captain – class – engage – farm – take – organic – plastic – shape

/ɑː/ as in car

/æ/ as in tap

/eɪ/ as in face

b. 63 **Listen and check your answers.**

MISSION CONTROL

Vers B1

SCENARIO Your vocational school organises a multilingual video contest called *#WeNeedAction* to support Earth Day on April 22nd.

MISSION EOC Create a one-minute video to celebrate Earth Day at school, promote environmental awareness and encourage your schoolmates to take action for nature.

1. **Cherchez** des informations sur la journée mondiale de la Terre : date, objectif, actions…
2. **Expliquez** pourquoi notre planète est en danger.
3. **Donnez** des conseils écocitoyens à vos amis : **proposez**-leur des actions simples à mettre en place dans leur vie quotidienne pour avoir un comportement plus écologique (*eco-friendly*).
4. **Précisez** ce qu'il se passera s'ils changent ou ne changent pas leurs habitudes.
5. **Trouvez** un slogan percutant pour terminer votre vidéo.
6. **Appuyez-vous** sur des images pour illustrer votre vidéo.
7. **Filmez-vous** en partageant équitablement le temps de parole. Vous pouvez utiliser Adobe Spark pour créer votre vidéo.

KEY QUESTION How can we bring humans and nature together? What do you think now?

Assess Yourself

Compétences de communication

- Décrire un évènement.
- Donner des recommandations.
- Décrire un futur hypothétique.

Compétences linguistiques

- Utiliser le lexique relatif à l'environnement (pollution, climat, gestes écocitoyens…).
- Exprimer des recommandations (impératif), la nécessité (*need to*) et l'absence d'obligation (*don't have to*).
- Exprimer la condition (*if*).

Compétences transversales

- Comprendre et respecter la consigne.
- Collaborer et coopérer.
- Être attentif au débit de sa voix et réaliser une vidéo de qualité.

Micro Project

- **Interdisciplinarité : parcours citoyen, enseignement professionnel**

ZERO WASTE WEEK PROJECT

You want to encourage people to be more eco-conscious.
You set up a zero waste week challenge at school, at home or at work.

1 Create your Project

1. **Get** in teams of 4 and **choose** your project: a zero waste week at school, at home or at work during your training period.
2. **Make** a list of 7 eco-friendly gestures you think are important and achievable.
3. **Explain** why these changes are necessary, what they will change. Give tips, figures…
4. **Create** the calendar promoting your zero waste week.

2 Present your Work

1. Show and present your creation to the rest of the class.
2. Vote for the best project in each category:
   - zero waste week at home;
   - zero waste week at school;
   - zero waste week in your company during your training period.

3 Act!

Try and respect the chosen calendar!

2022 April

Monday	Tuesday	Wednesday	Thursday	Friday	Saturday	Sunday
Zero waste snack 	Reduce paper use 	…	…	…	…	…

ZERO WASTE SNACKS

Instead of choosing packaged snacks, make your own (carrot sticks, apple slices, sandwiches…) or reach for a snack that doesn't have a lot of packaging. If you do so, you will limit the amount of waste you generate.

Accompagner • Personnaliser

Rendre compte en français de ce que je visionne

1. Identifier les stratégies

VIDEO
Youth & Climate: Jonathan, Drought in California / 1'43
www.lienmini.fr/40241-36

→ Method & Strategies
Tip 2 : Comprendre un support audio ou vidéo
Tip 6 : Rendre compte en français d'un support audio, vidéo ou écrit

Comprendre le support : repérer, déduire, identifier, associer

Lors du visionnage du document, **suivez** les étapes de la fiche Method & Strategies n° 2 et **trouvez** les informations principales : what? Who? Where? When? Why? How?

Préparer le compte-rendu : organiser, compléter, reformuler

Associez les items aux informations correspondantes. Puis **organisez** et **reformulez** l'essentiel du document pour en rendre compte.

1. La nature du document 2. Le thème 3. La source 4. Qui parle ? 5. Où ? 6. De quoi ? 7. De qui ? 8. Comment réagit-il/réagissent-ils ? 9. Pour quoi cette vidéo ?

a. *Jonathan, un jeune issu d'une famille d'agriculteurs.*
b. *Certains agriculteurs détruisent leurs récoltes par manque d'eau.*
c. *Cette vidéo vise à informer et dénoncer la situation.*
d. *Les images confirment ce que dit Jonathan.*
e. *La Californie/Watsonville.*
f. *La Californie nourrit en grande partie le pays.*
g. *Sans eau, la Californie serait un désert.*
h. *De sa famille.*
i. *Le témoignage d'un jeune homme.*
j. *Certains habitants de Californie envisagent de quitter la Californie pour trouver un nouvel emploi.*
k. *La sècheresse et ses conséquences.*
l. *Le narrateur veut agir pour protéger sa famille.*
m. *Alliance for Climate Education (ACE).*

Rédiger le compte-rendu : finaliser et structurer

Complétez le compte-rendu avec les éléments correspondants.

Introduction: Publié sur la chaine de l'organisation ..., la vidéo s'intitule "*Youth and Climate: Jonathan, drought in California*". Le document est un ... . Il évoque ... .

Contenu: Jonathan réside à ..., ville située dans l'état de ..., aux États-Unis. Il explique *d'abord* que la Californie souffre de ... depuis de nombreuses années. Il précise que la Californie ... . *Cependant,* sans eau, la Californie ... . Le narrateur se concentre *ensuite* sur la ville de ... et raconte l'histoire de sa famille. Jonathan est issu d'une famille de ... . *Aussi,* il explique que ... . *C'est pourquoi* il craint les conséquences de la sécheresse. *En effet,* de nombreuses personnes envisagent de... . Jonathan rapporte *également* des histoires sur des paysans qui ont détruit leurs récoltes *parce que* ... .

Conclusion: *Pour conclure,* Jonathan partage son propre ressenti par rapport à la situation. Il veut agir pour .... La vidéo montre des images qui ... les propos de Jonathan : on y voit des terrains arides, ainsi qu'une pancarte d'alerte sur un grillage. L'image du lac de Folsom est particulièrement marquante *car* elle montre que le lac s'est en grande partie asséché en 3 années. À travers l'histoire de Jonathan et de sa famille, cette vidéo vise à ... au regard de la pénurie d'eau que connait l'état de la Californie.

2. Appliquer

En vous appuyant sur la fiche Method & Strategies n° 6 et les stratégies que vous venez de mettre en œuvre, **rendez-compte** de la vidéo ci-contre. **Pensez** à réutiliser les mots de liaison en italique et les amorces de phrases soulignées dans le compte-rendu.

VIDEO
What is ACE? / 0'44
www.lienmini.fr/40241-37

Oser la mobilité professionnelle européenne

1. Comprendre les apports d'une mobilité

VIDEO
Erasmus+ 30 years anniversary - Tania Habimana, 27 (UK) / 0'31
www.lienmini.fr/40241-38

1 **Regardez** la vidéo et **expliquez** en anglais ce que l'expérience de mobilité avec Erasmus+ a apporté à Tania Habimana.

a. Regardez la vidéo sans le son.

1. *Jusqu'à 0'21.* **Décrivez** ce que vous voyez.

2. *De 0'21 à la fin.* **Précisez** en anglais : le lieu de vie, les études et le travail effectués par Tania Habimana ; le slogan choisi pour les 30 ans du programme Erasmus+.

b. Regardez la vidéo en entier avec le son.

1. Sélectionnez dans cette liste les « plus » apportés par l'expérience Erasmus+ à Tania.

discover other cultures - prepare exams - discover new skills - meet inspiring people - have business ideas - have a culture shock - be alone - feel at home everywhere - discover entrepreneurship

2. Répondez aux questions suivantes.

a. What did Tania Habimana study abroad? **b.** What did she discover and what did she learn?

c. How does she feel now?

TIPS

abroad: à l'étranger
entrepreneurship: l'entreprenariat
to feel at home: se sentir chez soi
to spring up: apparaitre, surgir

2 Connaissez-vous Tania Habimana ? **Faites** des recherches sur Internet et **découvrez** où elle est née, son parcours scolaire et universitaire, les pays dans lesquels elle a séjourné et ses succès. **Rédigez** en anglais un court texte pour la présenter et **expliquez** en quoi la mobilité a participé à son épanouissement personnel et professionnel.

2. Préparer ma mobilité professionnelle

1 **Choisissez** le pays dans lequel vous souhaiteriez vivre une expérience de mobilité. **Citez** en anglais au moins 10 éléments le concernant (localisation géographique, capitale, climat, nombre d'habitants, monnaie, monuments, sports nationaux, personnes célèbres...).

2 **Rendez-vous** sur le site officiel du tourisme de ce pays et **vérifiez** ces informations.

3. Oser

Vous prévoyez de réaliser votre période de formation en milieu professionnel à l'étranger.

1 En vous appuyant sur les « plus » de la mobilité indiqués par Tania Habimana, **expliquez** ce que vous attendez d'une telle expérience. **Utilisez** des expressions d'intention.

Exemple : I want to discover new cultures.
I intend to meet inspiring people.

2 **Préparez** également votre « checklist » afin de ne rien oublier avant votre départ.

Checklist Help!

- ✔ Make sure your passport and visa are up-to-date.
- ✔ Check for health advisories and travel warnings and advisories.
- ✔ Get vaccinations and bring photocopies of your prescriptions.
- ✔ Register your trip.
- ✔ Buy travel insurance.
- ✔ Pack appropriately...

UNIT 8 Make your

Vers B1

- Réseaux sociaux et Internet (pratiques et enjeux)

Look at the document and **describe** what you see. **Guess** what the teenagers are doing.

YOUR ROAD MAP

www.lienmini.fr/40241-39

UP TO YOU!

Easy Road
Extra Road
Bonus Road

KEY QUESTION How have mobile apps changed people's lives?

SCENARIO Surfing the Web, you read a post about useful apps for students and give an answer.

TASK 1 BE AN INFLUENCER **EE** Write a "what we like, what we don't like" post about an app.

TASK 2 JOIN THE CONVERSATION **EEI** Comment on a YouTube video about educational apps.

MISSION **EEI** Write a comment about apps.

Life APP-solutely Easy!

Open up!

1. Listen to the sound effects. What do they refer to?
2. Look at the screen of the mobile phone.
   a. **Match** each logo with the name of the corresponding app.
   Twitch – Sound Recorder – Twitter – Skype – Discord – Snapchat – YouTube – WhatsApp – Instagram – Messenger – Facebook
   b. **Find** the ones you hear in the recording.
   c. **Compare** with your partner.

WHAT ABOUT YOU?

1. **List** all the apps you have on your mobile phone.
2. **Classify** your 6 favourite ones, giving 6 points for your number 1, 5 points for your number 2...
3. **Make a chart** with the results of the whole class. What are the top 3 apps?

Get ready!

In-Class Activities

1. a. **Listen** and **repeat**.
   to surf the Web – to text – to download – to upload – to watch videos – to play – to chat – to share photos – to take pictures – to make phone calls – to talk to my friends – to put an alarm clock on – to receive phone calls – to listen to music – to record audio or videos – to take notes – to read books
   b. **Check** the meaning with an online dictionary if necessary.
2. a. **CHAIN SPEAKING GAME Use** this sentence starter and **complete** it with a verb from exercise 1.

   "With my phone, I can..."

   b. **Name** one of your classmates who will repeat your sentence, **add** another action and **name** another classmate. **Add** the last verb to be the winner!

By yourself!

Look at your phone. **List** the apps and **match** the verbs from exercise 1 which can be used with each of them.

What's Hot, What's Not!

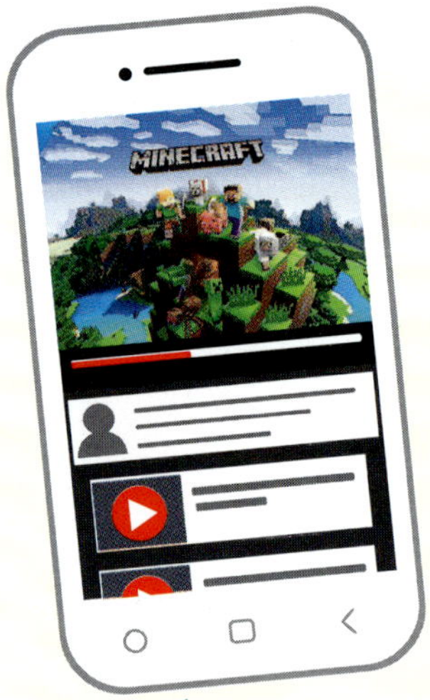

Hottest social Apps Trends for Teens
01 of 09 YouTube

What we like

- Huge variety of topics.
- Innumerable amount of videos.
- Can add commentary and reviews to videos.
- Can save videos to a watchlist for later viewing.

What we don't like

- Many videos have ads.
- YouTube has problems with commentary and child predators.
- No way to really filter undesirable video topics.

www.lifewire.com

➜ Method & Strategies
Tip 3 : Comprendre un support écrit

TIP
pics: contraction of *pictures*

1 **Look at the titles and the picture.**
a. What is this document about?
b. **Give** a title to each part.
c. **List** all you know about this app (topic – uses – features). **Complete** your list with your partner's ideas.

2 **Read the "what we like, what we don't like" article about YouTube.**
a. **List all the words which are close to French words.**
b. **Match the comments with their meaning.**
1. You can select videos to watch later.
2. Videos are about different subjects.
3. Children are not protected from inappropriate adult behaviours.
4. You can read or write comments about the video.
5. Videos are polluted by ads.

3 **Say if these elements about Snapchat are positive (+) or negative (–). Then, put them in the right label.**
a. If using location, can be intrusive.
b. Can take pictures or make videos.
c. Share your pics with friends or the public.
d. Available on mobile only.
e. Ads show up in the Discover part of the app.
f. Lots of filters and lenses making chatting fun.

What we like

What we don't like

WHAT ABOUT YOU?

1 **List the English words you use in French in social media language.**
Example: to chat.

2 **What are the positive and negative elements of your favourite app?**

“Either write something worth reading or do something worth writing.”
Benjamin Franklin

Extra Road Vers le Bac

4 **Discuss with your partner to find any other positive and negative elements about YouTube and Snapchat.**

TASK 1

BE AN INFLUENCER EE **Write a "what we like, what we don't like" post about an app.**

1 **Choose** an app and **write** a "what we like, what we don't like" post with a picture.

2 **Give** its name and its rank in the chart of your class.

Challenge yourself!

My Language Challenges	J'ai des difficultés ou je réponds non...
1. Je connais le vocabulaire des réseaux sociaux.	je fais le challenge n° 1.
2. Je suis capable de différencier *what* en tant que pronom relatif (que, ce que) ou pronom interrogatif (que, quel, quoi ?).	je fais le challenge n° 2.
3. Je sais prononcer correctement les mots contenant la lettre « u ».	je fais le challenge n° 3.
4. Je connais le sens des abréviations utilisées dans les réseaux sociaux.	je fais le challenge n° 4.

Challenge 4

Challenge 1 WORDS AND CULTURE Social Media Vocabulary

1 Take up the challenge!

Observez :

a. You can save videos to watchlist for later viewing.

b. Lots of filters and lenses making chatting fun are proposed in Snapchat.

- **Relevez dans ces phrases le champ lexical des réseaux sociaux.**
- **À quoi correspondent ces mots ?**

Play with Words and Culture n° 1

2 Find the word!

La plupart des mots associés aux réseaux sociaux et utilisés en français sont directement issus du lexique anglophone.

Exemple : The post of this influencer on Twitter has become viral. Haters and likers both share it on social media.

Enrichissez votre lexique en cherchant dans un dictionnaire le sens des mots suivants :

a. to register – to subscribe – to share – to browse – to lip-sync – to log in – to log out – to stalk – to swipe

b. a tag – a buzz – a comment – a follower – a hater – an influencer – a snap – a post – a story

Challenge 2 WORDS AND SENTENCES *What*: Relative Pronoun or Question Word?

1 Take up the challenge!

Observez :

a. What do you prefer in this app?

b. What we like in Snapchat is that we can add commentary and reviews to videos.

- **Que remarquez-vous sur la construction de chacune de ces phrases ?**
- **Comment traduiriez-vous *what* dans chacune des phrases ci-dessus ?**

2 Find the rule!

- ***What* peut être un pronom interrogatif (que... ? quel... ? quoi... ?) pour former une question :**
  ***What* + ... + sujet + ...**
- ***What* peut également être un pronom relatif (que, ce que) dans une phrase affirmative ou négative :**
  ***What* + sujet + ...**

RECAP > p. 126
Play with Words and Sentences n° 6

Challenge 3 WORDS AND SOUNDS The Letter "u"

1 Take up the challenge!

66 **Écoutez** les mots suivants :
YouTube – fun – huge – public – innumerable – using – undesirable – communication – pictures – intrusive – up – influencer

- **La lettre « u » se prononce-t-elle toujours de la même façon ?**
- **Classez** les mots selon la prononciation de cette lettre.

2 Find the sound!

La lettre « u » peut se prononcer :

- /ʌ/ comme dans ... ;
- /ju/ comme dans ... ;
- /u:/ comme dans ... ;
- /ʊ/ comme dans ... .

RECAP > p. 127
Play with Words and Sounds n° 10

Irregular Session

67 **Retrouvez** les trois verbes irréguliers *hear*, *spread* et *cost* dans le rabat à la fin du livre. **Écoutez**-les, **répétez**-les et **mémorisez**-les.

Cool Apps to Use

VIDEO
Top 10 Free Study Apps – Must have / 4'46
www.lienmini.fr/40241-40

→ Method & Strategies
Tip 2 : Comprendre un support audio ou vidéo

1 **Watch** the video from 0'31 to 0'57.
a. What type of video is it? b. What type of app is it about?

2 **Watch** again.
a. **Answer** the following questions.
1. What is the name of the app? 2. What is its topic?
3. What can you do with this app? 4. What are its positive elements?
5. Can you use this app if you have no Internet access?
6. How is this feature called? Is it a positive or a negative one?

b. **Look** at the Discord ID card and **build** this app ID card with the elements of the video.

3 **CLASS PUZZLE**
a. **Get into** groups to work on the app selected for you from the video.
1. Mathway [from 0'58 to 1'18] 2. Lingodeer [from 1'19 to 1'49]
3. Cold Turkey [from 1'50 to 2'41] 4. Quizlet [from 3'13 to 3'27]
5. Mindly [from 3'28 to 3'48]

b. **Watch** the part of the video corresponding to your group and **create** an ID card to describe the app.
c. In each group, **compare** your answers to get as many elements as you can about your video.
d. Each of you **joins** a different group, **presents** the app he/she has studied to the other students and **takes notes** about the other apps.

Extra Road Vers le Bac

4 **Watch** the presentation of School Planner app [from 0'07 to 0'30] and **create** the ID card for this new app.

Discord ID card

Name of the app: Discord
Topic: interaction with people
Uses/features: communicate via voice, video or text / media and files
Positive elements: easy to use / social skills when alone at home / streaming live to share contents

WHAT ABOUT YOU?

1 **Classify** the educational apps. Which one is your favourite? Why?

2 Do you know any other educational apps which can be useful? **Make** a list with your partners. Do you use them?

“Make sure you're happy in real life, not just for social media.”
Unknown

TASK 2

JOIN THE CONVERSATION EEI Comment on a YouTube video about educational apps.

1 **Read** the comments posted on this YouTube video (see Annex p. 113).

2 **Write** your own comment, saying which app(s) you would like to download and/or proposing a new educational app.

Challenge yourself!

My Language Challenges	J'ai des difficultés ou je réponds non...
1. Je connais le sens des adjectifs composés des suffixes *-ful* et *-less*.	je fais le challenge n° 1.
2. Je suis capable de former des adverbes avec le suffixe *-ly* et de les placer au bon endroit.	je fais le challenge n° 2.
3. Je sais accentuer les mots importants d'une phrase.	je fais le challenge n° 3.
4. Je connais les 5 grandes firmes américaines qui dominent le marché numérique.	je fais le challenge n° 4.

Challenge 4

Challenge 1 WORDS AND CULTURE Words Ending with *-ful* and *-less*

1 Take up the challenge!

Observez :

a. Thank you for sharing all these helpful apps!!! They're really useful!

b. When you search the Internet, the possibilities are endless.

- **Comment les mots soulignés sont-ils construits ?**
- **Que signifient-ils ?**

2 Find the word!

- **Ajouté à un nom, le suffixe ... (un seul « *l* ») forme un adjectif et indique l'abondance. Il provient de l'adjectif « *full* » (deux « *ll* »).**
  Exemple : powerful → puissant
- **Le suffixe ... marque la privation, l'absence (sans).**
  Exemple : useless → inutile

Play with Words and Culture n° 4 et 5

Challenge 2 WORDS AND SENTENCES Adverbs Ending with *-ly*

1 Take up the challenge!

Observez :

a. I personally love how this app is designed.

b. It is clearly the best app in my list.

c. This app is simply an online planner.

- **Quelle est la nature des mots soulignés ?**
- **Comment ces mots sont-ils composés ?**
- **Où sont-ils placés dans la phrase ?**

2 Find the rule!

- **Les adverbes peuvent être construits à partir d'adjectifs. Dans ce cas, on leur ajoute généralement la terminaison ... .**
- **L'adverbe est invariable et est généralement placé ... le verbe ou après l'auxiliaire « être ».**

RECAP > p. 126
Play with Words and Sentences n° 7, 8 et 9

Challenge 3 WORDS AND SOUNDS Sentence Stress

1 Take up the challenge!

68 **Écoutez** **la phrase suivante prononcée de trois façons différentes.**

I would definitely recommend this app.

- **Sur quel mot insiste-t-on lors de chaque écoute ?**
- **Pourquoi ?**

Play with Words and Sounds n° 11 et 12

2 Find the sound!

Dans une phrase, on accentue les mots importants en fonction du message que l'on veut transmettre :

- *I would definitely recommend this app* : j'insiste sur ..., car c'est la personne qui parle qui recommande cette appli (et pas une autre).
- *I would definitely recommend this app* : j'insiste sur ..., car après réflexion, pas de doute, c'est bien une appli à recommander.
- *I would definitely recommend this app* : j'insiste sur ..., car c'est cette appli qu'il faut avoir (et pas une autre).

Irregular Session

69 **Retrouvez** les trois verbes irréguliers ***ring***, ***choose*** et ***draw*** dans le rabat à la fin du livre. **Écoutez**-les, **répétez**-les et **mémorisez**-les. **Révisez** les trois verbes appris précédemment.

Play with...

WORDS AND CULTURE

1 a. **Complete** the following sentences with the appropriate word from the list.

app – vlog – meme – haters – influencers

1. Famous social media personalities who have many followers are called ... .
2. ... on social media are people who post some negative comments in order to criticise somebody's success.
3. My favourite ... is Snapchat because I can share my pics with my friends.
4. A ... is a form of blog composed of a set of videos that someone regularly posts on the Internet.
5. When a video, picture or phrase is spread widely on the Internet for humorous effect, it is called a ... .

b. **What does an influencer do? Write** as many actions as you can about what he/she does.

2 a. **Match** the SMS abbreviations with their meaning.

1.

OMG – AMA – gr8 – IRL – FYI – 2nite – FAQ – BFF – ASAP – C&P – B2W

2.

in real life – frequently asked questions – as soon as possible – oh my god! – back to work – copy and paste – ask me anything – best friend forever – tonight – for your information – great

b. **Read** the messages and **rewrite** them in a complete sentence.

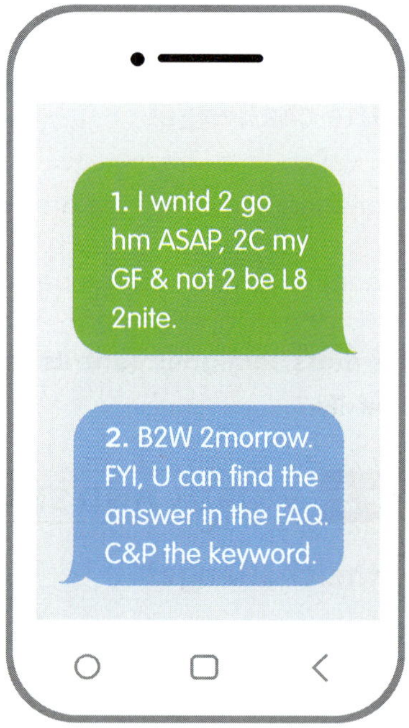

3 **Write** a text message to your classmate. He/She will text you back.

4 In each sentence, **turn** the noun into an adjective using the right suffix.

a. This story continues forever, it is end... .

b. If a part of your body is pain..., it hurts a lot.

c. This girl has got millions of followers. Indeed, she is beauti... .

d. Be very care... about what you post online as it could be dangerous.

e. This influencer is fear..., he is not afraid of anything.

5 a. **Turn** the 6 nouns into adjectives using *-ful* or *-less*.

use – help – taste – colour – power – hope

b. **Write** 6 sentences using these adjectives.

WORDS AND SENTENCES

6 **These sentences are written with no punctuation. For each of them, say if *what* is an interrogative or a relative pronoun and write the punctuation. Then, translate the sentences.**

a. Keeping in touch with my friends is exactly what I like with Messenger

b. What is your favourite app

c. What teenagers prefer is pretty hard to say because they change every day

d. What do you want me to post on Twitter

7 a. **Turn the following adjectives into adverbs.**

soft *sudden* *recent* *quick* *gradual* *frequent* *strong* *extreme*

b. **Choose** an appropriate adverb and **put** it in the right place in the following sentences.

1. You fall asleep to your favourite music with Sleep Timer.

2. The app stopped working.

3. I will re-install the app.

4. This app is my favourite one.

8 **Find** as many adverbs ending with *-ly* as possible. You've got 3 minutes!

3 min

9 **Write** 3 short sentences using adverbs ending with *-ly*.

WORDS AND SOUNDS

10 70 a. **Listen** to the words and **classify** them according to the pronunciation of the letter "u".

helpful - study - educational - useless - students - feature - influencer - subscribe - buzz - subjects - polluted - public

b. Now, **read** the words. Your classmate will **check** your pronunciation.

11 71 **Listen** and **match** the translation with the sentence you hear.

1. Chacune des applications est vraiment intéressante, quelle qu'elle soit.

2. Chaque application est intéressante dans son propre domaine.

3. Chaque application est vraiment parfaite dans son domaine.

12 **Choose** what you want to mean with this sentence, then **read** it to your partner who has to **find** which is the element you want to insist on.

WhatsApp is the most popular chat application in the world.

a. L'application de conversation écrite la plus célèbre s'appelle WhatsApp.

b. WhatsApp est la meilleure application de conversation écrite.

c. WhatsApp est la meilleure application dans le monde entier.

MISSION CONTROL

Vers B1

SCENARIO Surfing the Web, you read a post about useful apps for students and give an answer.

MISSION EEI Write a comment about apps.

1. **Lisez** ce post et **trouvez** des informations concernant :
   - le problème rencontré par l'auteur ;
   - la raison pour laquelle il veut connaitre les applications françaises ;
   - l'objectif de ses questions.
2. **Trouvez** les 4 questions posées par l'étudiant pour adapter votre réponse.
3. **Sélectionnez** 2 ou 3 applications différentes que vous utilisez souvent.
4. **Préparez** votre post :
   - **expliquez** ce que vous pouvez faire avec ces applications et **précisez** leurs avantages et leurs inconvénients ;
   - **enrichissez** votre réponse en utilisant des adjectifs en *-less* et/ou *-ful* et des adverbes en *-ly*.
5. **Rédigez** votre commentaire et **vérifiez** que vous avez répondu aux 4 questions de ce post.

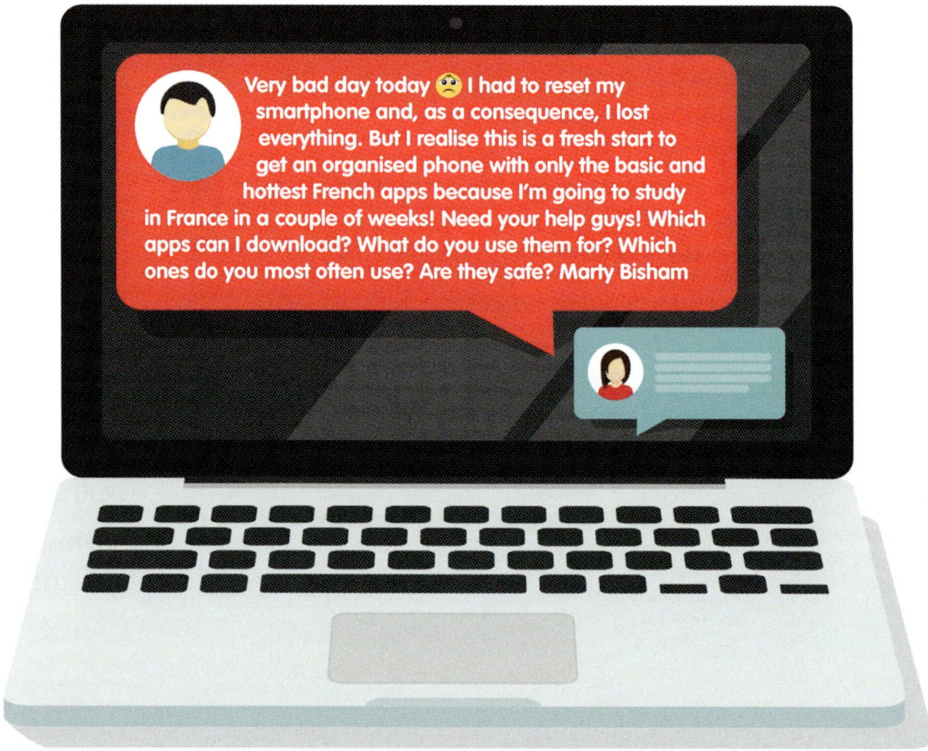

KEY QUESTION How have mobile apps changed people's lives? What do you think now?

Assess Yourself

Compétences de communication

- Comprendre un post sur un réseau social.
- Présenter les utilisations, les avantages et les dangers d'une application.
- Contribuer à une discussion en ligne et publier un commentaire personnel.

Compétences linguistiques

- Comprendre et utiliser le lexique lié à la thématique des applications et des réseaux sociaux.
- Enrichir les phrases avec des adverbes en *-ly* et les placer correctement.
- Enrichir les phrases d'adjectifs avec les suffixes *-ful* et *-less*.

Compétences transversales

- Comprendre et respecter la consigne.
- Prendre en compte le message reçu.
- Respecter la forme d'un commentaire de réseau social et soigner sa présentation.

Exam Road

COMPRÉHENSION DE L'ORAL

Visionnez le document trois fois. Puis **rendez compte** en français du document. **Précisez :**

- la nature et le thème principal du document ;
- l'intérêt / la fiabilité de cette étude ;
- des exemples d'utilisation des réseaux sociaux par les adolescents ;
- les points positifs et négatifs des réseaux sociaux cités par les adolescents ;
- l'utilisation que les adolescents font de ces réseaux sociaux.

CE EE

VIDEO How Teens Use Social Media / 1'31 www.lienmini.fr/40241-41

Concluez votre compte-rendu en expliquant la fonction du document : s'agit-il d'informer, de convaincre, de critiquer, de dénoncer ou de divertir ?

EXPRESSION ORALE EN CONTINU

Présentez et **rendez compte** en anglais (en 3 minutes minimum) du projet réalisé autour des applications et des réseaux sociaux. Pour organiser votre prise de parole, vous pourrez indiquer :

- quelle était votre connaissance du sujet avant de l'étudier en classe ;
- ce que vous avez appris concernant le sujet ;
- quel était l'objectif du projet ;
- quelles étapes vous ont amené à réussir la mission ;
- quelle partie vous avez préférée / le moins appréciée dans ce projet ;
- quelles difficultés vous avez rencontrées et comment vous les avez surmontées ;
- ce que ce projet vous a apporté d'un point de vue personnel et/ou professionnel.

Pensez à donner des exemples !

Rappel : l'attendu au baccalauréat sera de 5 minutes.

EXPRESSION ORALE EN INTERACTION

72 **Écoutez** les questions et **enregistrez** vos réponses.

a. Soyez attentif au mot interrogatif utilisé dans la question.

b. Si vous utilisez dans vos réponses des mots de la question, vérifiez de bien les prononcer en vous basant sur le modèle entendu.

c. Justifiez vos réponses par des exemples.

Accompagner • Personnaliser

Échanger par courriel

→ Method & Strategies
Tip 7 : Interagir à l'écrit

1. Observer

Thomas vient de recevoir le courriel ci-dessous de sa correspondante Amy, lycéenne à Portsmouth.

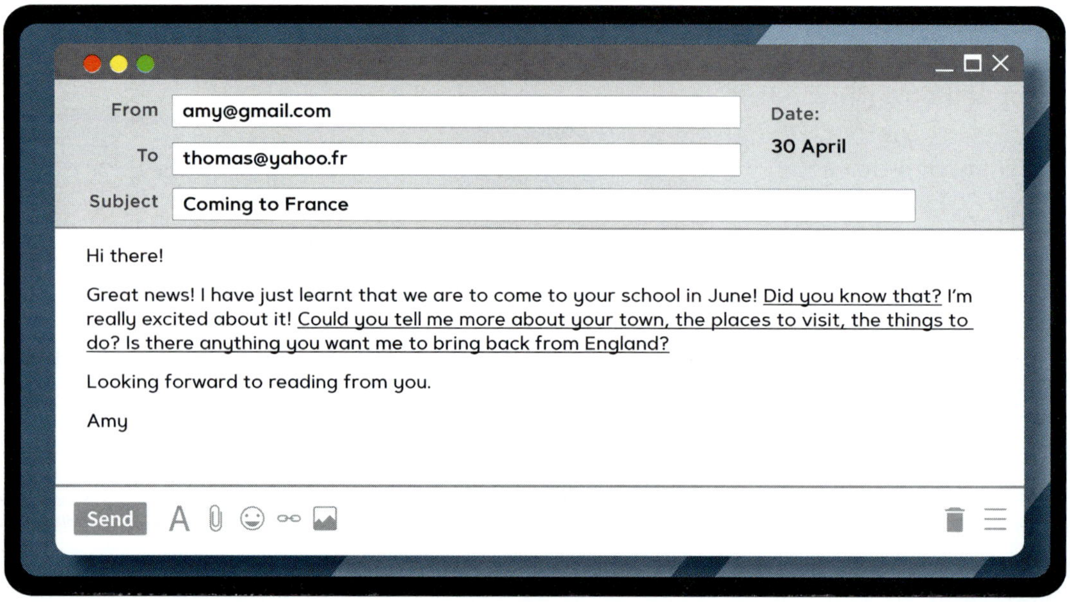

From: amy@gmail.com
To: thomas@yahoo.fr
Subject: Coming to France
Date: 30 April

Hi there!

Great news! I have just learnt that we are to come to your school in June! <u>Did you know that?</u> I'm really excited about it! <u>Could you tell me more about your town, the places to visit, the things to do? Is there anything you want me to bring back from England?</u>

Looking forward to reading from you.

Amy

Send

1 **Prenez connaissance** des supports élaborés par Thomas pour rédiger sa réponse et **observez** sa méthode de travail.

Document 1 : le courrier reçu

→ **L'expéditeur** : Amy / **La date** : 15 April / **Le sujet** : coming to France

→ **Les mots importants** : to your school / in June / your town / visit / things to do

→ **Les questions** : soulignées

Document 2 : mes idées et mon plan

Réponses à apporter : I didn't know about the trip; places to visit; things to do; things to bring back from England...

Questions à poser : about the trip : when? how long? where (sleep)? other things to do?

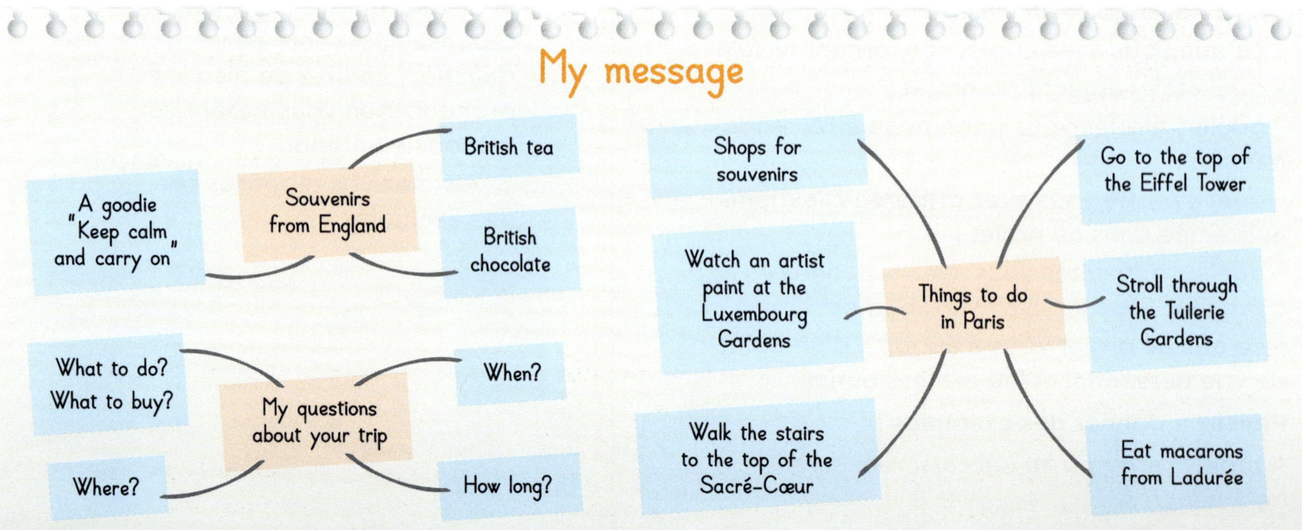

2 **Lisez** son courriel.

Document 3 : ma réponse

From: thomas@yahoo.fr

To: amy@gmail.com

Subject: Your trip to France

Date: 4 May

Hello Amy,

This is really fantastic! I didn't know about your trip to France! I'm looking forward to meeting you! I'm really excited about it! I've got so many questions to ask: when exactly will you arrive and how long will you stay? Where will you stay: in families or at school?

Let me tell you about what we can do with our classmates in Paris: we can go to the top of the Eiffel Tower, stroll through the Tuilerie Gardens, walk the stairs to the top of the Sacré-Coeur. We can also eat macarons from Ladurée. It may be possible to watch an artist paint at the Luxembourg Gardens as well. Of course we will shop for souvenirs. Any ideas of what you would like to buy in Paris? By the way, I would appreciate tasting some British tea and chocolate or having a British "Keep calm and carry on" postcard.

Let us know if there are other things you would like to do or discover in Paris!

See you next month! XOXOXX!

Thomas

Send

2. Identifier les stratégies

En vous aidant de la fiche **Method & Strategies n° 7** et des supports élaborés par Thomas, **retrouvez** et **identifiez** les étapes et les stratégies mises en œuvre.

a. Dans le document 1, **repérez** les éléments relevés par Thomas pour identifier la thématique, comprendre ce qui est attendu et trouver les informations à transmettre.

b. Dans le document 2, **repérez** la forme retenue par Thomas pour lister les éléments à transmettre et les questions à poser.

c. Dans le message rédigé (document 3) :

1. **Associez** les réponses de Thomas aux questions posées par Amy. Quel est l'auxiliaire utilisé pour parler de ce qu'il est possible de faire à Paris ?
2. **Observez** les questions posées par Thomas. À quel temps sont-elles formulées ? Comment le savez-vous ?

d. Dans les messages de Amy et de Thomas, **repérez** :

1. les caractéristiques d'un courriel, les formules d'ouverture et autres expressions spécifiques ;
2. les expressions qui montrent leur enthousiasme.

3. Appliquer

Appuyez-vous sur la fiche **Method & Strategies n° 7** pour rédiger la réponse de Amy à Thomas (80 à 100 mots minimum).

a. **Préparez** votre courriel en vous inspirant des documents 1 et 2.

b. **Comparez** votre travail à celui effectué par Thomas dans le document 3 et **enrichissez** votre réponse. **Veillez** à respecter la forme attendue lors de l'envoi d'un message électronique.

U1
3
p. 14

Year 11 – School Timetable

Period	Monday	Tuesday	Wednesday	Thursday	Friday
8:30 am - 8:50 am	Assembly	Assembly	Assembly	Assembly	Assembly
Period 1 9:00 am - 9:50 am	Science S23	French L5	Maths S11	English L13	History L36
BREAK					
Period 2 10 am - 10:50 am	IT T7	Maths S11	IT T7	French L5	Science S23
BREAK					
Period 3 11:00 - 11:50	English L13	English L13	IT T7	Science S23	Science S23
LUNCH					
Period 4 12:30 am - 1:20 pm	PE	IT T7	English L13	Maths S11	Maths S11
BREAK					
Period 5 1:30 pm - 2:20 pm	PE	IT T7	History L36	IT T7	Maths S11
BREAK					
Period 6 2:30 pm - 3:20 pm	PLP	Unscheduled teachers available for one-to-one and group support	Unscheduled teachers available for one-to-one and group support	PLP	Unscheduled teachers available for one-to-one and group support
BREAK					
3:40 pm - 5:30 pm	Optional after-school club activity	Optional after-school club activity	Optional after-school club activity	Optional after-school club activity	Optional after-school club activity

NB : PLP : Personal Learning Plan.

U2
TASK 1
p. 24

3:30 am: get up

3:45 am: meditate

4:15 am: get prepped for the day ahead

4:30 am: go running

5:30 am: have breakfast (2 eggs and oatmeal)

6:00 am: start his workout routine (lift weights, do squats, do pullups, run on a treadmill...)

1:00 pm: drive to set in his pickup truck

00:00 am: go to bed

Have 5 to 7 meals a day / eat 12 eggs a day

Have a rest on Sunday

Adapted from https://owaves.com

U5
TASK 1
p. 62

US national day ID card

Name: Independence Day

Date: 4th July

Origins: historical

Original event: Declaration of Independence in 1776

Symbols: American flag / fireworks / parades / bonfire

U6
TASK 1
p. 76

U8
TASK 2
p. 104

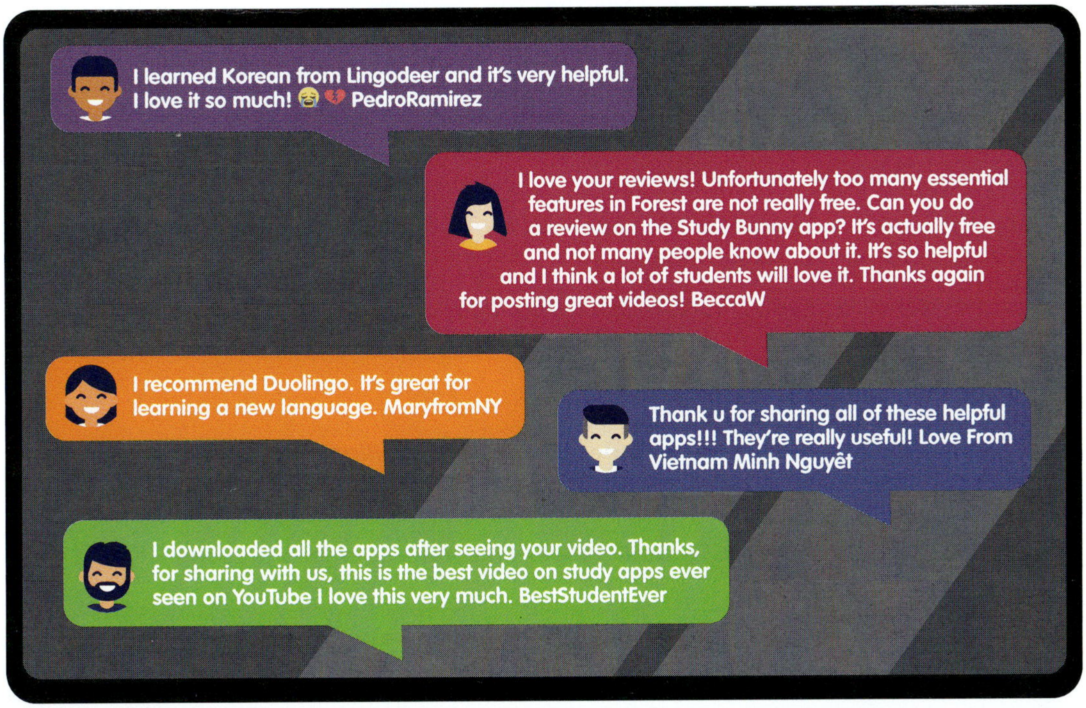

Tip 1 : Apprendre à mémoriser le lexique

Contextualiser

- **Associez** à une image (*flashcard*, diaporama…), un geste, un moment, une personne, un lieu, un objet… → *intelligences kinesthésique et visuelle*
- **Rapprochez** des mots que vous connaissez (en français, dans les autres langues apprises, dans les langues de la maison) et **classez** (familles de mots, synonymes, contraires…). → *intelligence du naturaliste*

Mémoriser la phonie

- **Imitez, répétez** à voix haute/basse/dans votre tête ; **tapez** des mains sur la syllabe accentuée ; **enregistrez**-vous, puis **écoutez-vous** ; **faites dire** par quelqu'un d'autre, puis répétez ; **faites rimer** avec d'autres mots connus. → *intelligences rythmique et intrapersonnelle*
- « **Photographiez** », puis **fermez** les yeux en « revoyant » ce qui est à apprendre. → *intelligence visuelle*
- **Soyez attentif** à la façon dont vous **formez** les mots avec votre bouche. → *intelligence kinesthésique*
- **Répétez** ces activités à deux, en groupe et **corrigez**-vous entre pairs. → *intelligence interpersonnelle*
- **Jouez** → *intelligence interpersonnelle :*

Kim's game	Chinese whisper	Chain conversation	Spot the odd one out	Family game
L'image correspondant à un mot disparait dans une série d'images. Soyez le premier à le retrouver et prononcez-le !	Transmettez à voix haute un mot à votre partenaire, qui doit à son tour le transmettre en respectant fidèlement le modèle.	À partir d'un thème, répétez la liste de mots entendue et ajoutez-en un.	Trouvez l'intrus dans une série d'images, de mots, de mimes… et prononcez-le !	Retrouvez les différents mots d'une même famille.

Astuces

- ***Assurez-vous*** *de comprendre avant d'apprendre.*
- ***Créez*** *des liens entre ce que vous souhaitez mémoriser et des moments de vie (évènements, lieux, moments, personnes, objets…).*
- ***Appuyez-vous*** *sur vos intelligences multiples : intelligence verbale (ou linguistique), rythmique (ou musicale), kinesthésique (ou corporelle), visuelle (ou spatiale), logique (ou mathématique), interpersonnelle, intrapersonnelle, du naturaliste. Multipliez les approches (images, sons, gestes…), seul ou en groupe !*
- ***Associez*** *les sons du mot et le sens avant d'associer l'écriture au mot.* ***Travaillez*** *la phonie avant la graphie.*
- ***Manipulez*** *le lexique en contexte.*
- ***Répétez*** *pour fixer !*
- ***Ayez confiance*** *en vos capacités.*

Associer la phonie à la graphie

- **Associez** l'écrit à la prononciation : **épelez, recopiez, effacez** au fur et à mesure, puis **reconstituez.** → *intelligences verbale et visuelle*
- **Lisez** plusieurs fois à voix haute/basse. → *intelligences verbale et rythmique*

Mémoriser à long terme

- **Intégrez** les mots à apprendre dans des énoncés. → *intelligence verbale*
- **Repérez** un virelangue et **répétez**-le. → *intelligence rythmique*
- **Mimez, jouez,** puis **partagez.** → *intelligences kinesthésique, intrapersonelle et interpersonnelle*
- **Réactivez** en revoyant les mots régulièrement ; **renouvelez** les activités si nécessaire. → *intelligences multiples*

D'autres stratégies pour mémoriser des énoncés, des textes et votre leçon dans votre Bonus Road ! Tips

Tip 2 : Comprendre un support audio ou vidéo

Anticiper lors de la première écoute/du premier visionnage

1. **Prenez connaissance** du titre, du support, de la source, de la date.
2. **Appuyez-vous** sur le contexte, les images, la musique…
3. **Identifiez** les différents interlocuteurs, la tonalité du message.
4. **Repérez** les indices d'espace et de temps.
5. **Mobilisez** vos connaissances.

Objectifs **Anticiper** sur le sujet, **identifier la nature du document** (message, interview, présentation professionnelle, récit, documentaire, journal télévisé, émission…), **le contexte de communication** (vie professionnelle ou vie personnelle, citoyenne…), **et le thème, faire des hypothèses** (sur l'intention du message, les sentiments et réactions des locuteurs, la situation dans l'espace et le temps, le contenu…).

Astuces

Pour être dans une posture d'écoute favorable :
- *soyez attentif ;*
- *concentrez-vous sur ce que vous connaissez (et non ce qui est inconnu) ;*
- *mémorisez le connu ;*
- *ne cherchez pas nécessairement à tout comprendre ;*
- *ayez confiance en vos capacités.*

Pour mieux vous organiser : *prenez des notes au fur et à mesure des différents visionnages ou écoutes. Pensez à sauter des lignes et laisser de l'espace pour compléter vos notes à chaque écoute.*

Repérer, déduire, identifier, associer lors des écoutes ou visionnages successifs

Deuxième écoute ou visionnage

1. **Repérez** les noms propres, les indications chiffrées, les lieux, puis les mots connus.
2. **Déduisez** le sens des mots inconnus grâce à leur transparence, leur racine, suffixe ou préfixe.

Objectifs **Identifier** la situation de communication, **déduire** le type d'informations données, **faire des hypothèses** à partir de ces éléments (qui ? à qui ? quand ? où ? quoi ?) et les **mémoriser**.

Écoutes ou visionnages suivants

1. **Concentrez-vous** sur les mots accentués.
2. **Repérez** les répétitions, les champs lexicaux.
3. **Notez** les mots-clés.
4. **Déduisez** le sens des mots inconnus à partir du contexte.
5. **Repérez** les marques orales de conjugaison, les marqueurs de temps et les connecteurs.

Objectifs **Repérer** les mots porteurs de sens, **dégager** les idées principales, **trouver** les liens entre les idées (ordre des faits, situation dans le temps, arguments, cause/conséquence/but/contraste…), faire d'autres hypothèses (quoi ? comment ? pourquoi ?) et/ou **affiner** les hypothèses précédentes. **Sélectionner**, **classer** et **associer** les informations importantes.

Compléter et vérifier lors de la dernière écoute/du dernier visionnage

1. **Cherchez** les éléments subjectifs (adjectifs, adverbes, modaux…) et les expressions d'opinion.
2. **Concentrez-vous** sur les détails qui vous manquent.
3. **Relisez et vérifiez** vos prises de notes.

Objectifs **Confirmer** les réactions ou intentions des locuteurs, **identifier** l'objectif du document, **vérifier** les hypothèses, **s'assurer** de la compréhension.

Useful Words and Sentences, p. 123

Tip 3 : Comprendre un support écrit

Anticiper avant la première lecture

1. **Appuyez-vous** sur les indices non verbaux, le paratexte, l'organisation du support (source, illustrations, titre, date, paragraphes, alinéas...).
2. **Mobilisez** vos connaissances.

Objectifs **Anticiper** sur le sujet ; **identifier** la nature du document (message, récit, article de journal, publicité, petite annonce, courrier personnel ou professionnel, notice, mode d'emploi...), le contexte de communication (vie professionnelle ou vie personnelle, citoyenne...) et éventuellement la date et le lieu de publication ; **découvrir** le thème ; **faire des hypothèses** sur le contenu.

Astuces

Adoptez une posture de lecture active :

- *soyez attentif ;*
- *concentrez-vous sur ce que vous connaissez (et non ce qui est inconnu). Surlignez ce que vous connaissez ;*
- *mémorisez le connu ;*
- *posez-vous des questions ;*
- *modifiez vos hypothèses si elles se révèlent inexactes.*

Pour mieux vous repérer, *utilisez des couleurs et des outils de repérage : entourer, souligner, surligner, cocher....*

Repérer, déduire, identifier, associer lors des lectures successives

Première lecture

1. **Repérez** les noms propres, les indications chiffrées, les sigles..., puis les mots connus ou transparents.
2. **Déduisez** le sens des éléments inconnus à partir des éléments connus, des suffixes, des préfixes.

Objectifs **Identifier** la situation de communication, **déduire** le type d'informations données, **faire des hypothèses** (qui ? à qui ? quand ? où ? quoi ?) et les **mémoriser**.

Lectures suivantes

1. **Repérez** les répétitions, les champs lexicaux.
2. **Notez** les mots-clés et **identifiez** les verbes d'action.
3. **Déduisez** le sens des mots inconnus à partir du contexte.
4. **Repérez** les marques de conjugaison, les marqueurs de temps et les connecteurs.

Objectifs **Dégager** les idées principales, **trouver** les liens logiques entre les idées (ordre des faits, arguments, cause/conséquence/but/contraste...) et les personnages, **situer** dans le temps (passé, présent, futur), **faire d'autres hypothèses** (quoi ? comment ? pourquoi ?) et/ou affiner les hypothèses précédentes. **Sélectionner, classer** et **mettre en relation** les informations importantes.

Approfondir et vérifier lors de la dernière lecture

1. **Cherchez** les éléments subjectifs (adjectifs, adverbes, modaux...) et les expressions d'opinion.
2. **Concentrez-vous** sur les détails qui vous manquent.
3. **Relisez** et **vérifiez** vos notes.

Objectifs **Identifier** le point de vue de l'auteur et des personnages, l'objectif du document, **vérifier** les hypothèses et **s'assurer** de la compréhension.

Useful Words and Sentences, p. 123

Tip 4 : S'exprimer à l'oral

Anticiper en amont de votre production

1. **Lisez** attentivement la consigne et surlignez les mots importants.
2. **Mobilisez** le lexique, les contenus culturels et professionnels connus.
3. **Effectuez** les recherches nécessaires pour obtenir les informations manquantes.
4. **Choisissez vos outils et modalités de travail :** plan, sommaire, fiche, carte mentale, organigramme, diaporama...

Objectifs **Identifier** le contexte et la thématique dans lesquels le sujet se situe (vie professionnelle ou vie personnelle, citoyenne...) et **comprendre** ce qui est attendu (raconter, décrire, présenter, rendre compte, donner son avis...).

Astuces

Pour s'adresser efficacement à un auditoire :

- *planifiez votre prise de parole ;*
- *osez prendre la parole ;*
- *placez-vous en position de communication au sein du groupe ;*
- *pensez à l'effet que vous voulez produire sur ceux qui vous écoutent ;*
- *adaptez votre discours à la situation et à l'auditoire.*

Noter, structurer, oraliser lors de la préparation de votre prise de parole

Préparation

1. Sans rédiger, **notez** vos idées et des exemples pour les illustrer.
2. **Structurez, reformulez et inspirez-vous** de modèles connus.
3. **Organisez** votre propos (introduction, deux ou trois parties, conclusion).
4. **Choisissez** un document iconographique (photographie, schéma, croquis, reproduction d'œuvre d'art, etc.).

Objectifs **Construire** votre propos, **organiser** votre prise de parole, **illustrer** votre travail.

Mise en voix

1. **Exprimez-vous en réduisant** progressivement votre support à un plan, une carte mentale, un sommaire ou quelques mots-clés.
2. **Entrainez-vous** à prononcer les mots difficiles et à respecter l'intonation.

Objectifs Vous **détacher** de vos notes, **respecter** les règles de la prononciation, **employer** l'intonation appropriée.

Réussir la prise de parole

1. **Appuyez-vous** sur le support préparé pour votre intervention ainsi que le document iconographique choisi.
2. **Utilisez** des *gap-fillers* et des stratégies de contournement en cas de difficultés (définition, synonyme...).
3. **Regardez** votre auditoire ; **appuyez-vous** sur le non-verbal (posture, gestuelle, mimiques...).
4. **Articulez** clairement, **adaptez** votre voix et votre débit de parole.

Objectifs **Accompagner** votre prise de parole, **surmonter** les difficultés, vous **reprendre**, vous **autocorriger**, **obtenir** l'attention.

Vérifier après la prise de parole

1. **Écoutez** vos camarades et **corrigez** leurs erreurs.
2. **Acceptez** les conseils et remarques qu'ils peuvent vous donner en vous écoutant.
3. **Listez** les erreurs que vous commettez souvent pour apprendre à les éviter.

Objectifs Vous **intercorriger**, **pallier** vos difficultés, **consolider** vos acquis.

→ **FLAP:** Pronunciation
→ **FLAP:** Opinions, Linking Words and Gap Fillers

Useful Words and Sentences, p. 123

METHOD & STRATEGIES

Tip 5 : S'exprimer à l'écrit

Anticiper en amont de votre production

1. **Lisez** attentivement la consigne/le sujet et **surlignez** les mots importants.
2. **Mobilisez** le lexique et les expressions connus en lien avec la thématique, ainsi que les contenus culturels ou professionnels nécessaires.
3. **Effectuez** les recherches nécessaires pour obtenir les informations manquantes.
4. **Choisissez** vos outils et modalités de travail : plan, sommaire, fiche, carte mentale, organigramme, diaporama...

Objectifs **Identifier** le contexte et la thématique dans lesquels le sujet se situe (vie personnelle, quotidienne, sociale et citoyenne ou vie professionnelle), **comprendre** ce qui est attendu (décrire un évènement, écrire une histoire, un texte sur un sujet familier ou actuel, rendre compte d'une expérience, réagir à une problématique d'ordre général, commenter une citation ou une affirmation...).

Astuces

- **Planifiez** *votre travail.*
- **Compensez** *lorsque le lexique vous manque.*
- **Appuyez-vous** *sur votre expérience personnelle ou professionnelle.*
- **Réagissez** *et* **donnez** *votre opinion.*
- **Recommencez** *différemment si vous rencontrez des difficultés.*
- **Corrigez** *vos maladresses et vos erreurs.*

Noter, rédiger, structurer, enrichir lors de votre passage à l'écrit

Préparation

1. **Réfléchissez** à votre plan.
2. **Notez** vos idées sous forme de mots-clés ou d'énoncés brefs en vous appuyant sur les outils et modalités de travail choisis.
3. **Pensez** à des exemples pour illustrer votre propos.

Objectifs **Rassembler** vos idées et les **organiser**.

Rédaction de vos différents jets d'écriture

PHASE 1

1. **Rédigez et structurez** vos énoncés ; **utilisez** des tournures que vous maitrisez (questions, réponses connues...). **Soyez attentif** aux temps, à la grammaire.
2. **Préparez** votre introduction et votre conclusion.

Objectifs **Rédiger** vos énoncés, **structurer** votre propos, **organiser** votre production.

PHASE 2

3. **Variez** le lexique et les structures.
4. **Ajoutez** des mots de liaison (connecteurs logiques, chronologiques, spatiaux...).

Objectifs **Enrichir** vos phrases, **mettre en évidence** les liens logiques entre vos idées.

Vérifier votre écrit

1. **Relisez** attentivement votre écrit.
2. **Vérifiez** l'orthographe, la grammaire, la ponctuation, le nombre de mots...

Objectif Vous **autocorriger**.

→ **FLAP:** Opinions, Linking Words and Gap Fillers

Useful Words and Sentences, p. 123

Tip 6 : Rendre compte en français d'un support audio, vidéo ou écrit

Comprendre le support : repérer, déduire, identifier, associer

Suivez les étapes proposées dans la fiche Method & Strategies n° 2 ou la fiche Method & Strategies n° 3 selon la situation, **identifiez** les indices non verbaux et le paratexte et **trouvez** les informations principales : *What? Who? Where? When? Why? How?*

Objectifs **Identifier** la nature du document et le thème principal du document, **repérer et dégager** les informations et idées principales.

Astuces

- *Mettez-vous en posture d'écoute ou de lecture active !*
- *Soyez attentif, efficace et organisé !*
- *Faites une liste des informations à indiquer (qui, que, quoi...) et barrez celles que vous traitez au fur et à mesure.*
- *Ne cherchez pas à traduire mot à mot ce que vous avez compris ! Reformulez l'essentiel du document.*
- *Soyez objectif ! Ne donnez pas votre opinion sur la thématique du document ! Vous pouvez cependant conclure en indiquant les intentions de l'auteur/du locuteur.*

Préparer le compte-rendu : organiser, reformuler

1. **Répondez** en français aux questions suivantes :
   - *Quelle* est la nature du document ? *Quel* en est le thème ? *Quelle* en est la source ?
   - *Qui* parle ? *de qui ?*
   - *Où* se passe l'action ? *Quels* sont les lieux évoqués ?
   - *Quand* se passe l'action ? *Quelles* sont les périodes/moments évoqués ?
   - *Quelle* est la situation ? *Quels* sont les informations ou faits importants ?
   - *Comment* sont présentés/perçus les informations, les évènements, les faits ? *Que* pensent les personnes, le locuteur, l'auteur ? *Quel message* les images véhiculent-elles ?
   - *Pourquoi* le locuteur/l'auteur s'exprime-t-il ? *Quels* sont ses objectifs, intentions ? Cherche-t-il à raconter, informer, convaincre, critiquer, dénoncer, divertir, etc. ?
2. **Organisez** vos notes.

Objectifs **Reformuler** l'essentiel du document et en **rendre compte** en français en précisant : la nature, la source et le thème principal du document ; la situation, les informations ou faits importants ; l'identité des personnes ou personnages et leurs liens ; les différents points de vue ; les éventuels éléments implicites du document ; la fonction et la portée du document (relater, informer, convaincre, critiquer, dénoncer, divertir, etc.).

Rédiger le compte-rendu : finaliser, structurer

1. **Préparez** une introduction : nature, source, thème.
2. **Rédigez** le corps du compte-rendu : faits, arguments, détails.
3. **Proposez** un dernier paragraphe ou une conclusion : point de vue, portée.

Objectifs **Rédiger** un compte-rendu structuré, **dire** en quoi le support est intéressant et quel est son objectif.

Compléter, vérifier

1. **Relisez, écoutez** ou **visionnez** à nouveau le document support et votre compte-rendu.
2. **Soyez attentif** à la correction de la langue française.

Objectifs **Vérifier** l'exactitude des informations transmises et **compléter** le compte-rendu. **Corriger** le texte rédigé en français si besoin.

Useful Words and Sentences, p. 123

Tip 7 : Interagir à l'écrit

Anticiper en amont de votre production

1. **Lisez attentivement** le sujet ou le message.
2. **Repérez** les informations reçues/connues : expéditeur, destinataire, date, sujet...
3. **Surlignez** les mots importants.
4. **Repérez** les questions directes ou indirectes.
5. **Mobilisez** vos connaissances (lexique, grammaire, culture...).
6. **Effectuez** les recherches ou demandes nécessaires pour obtenir les informations manquantes.

Objectifs **Identifier** le contexte dans lequel le sujet se situe (vie quotidienne, personnelle, sociale et citoyenne ou vie professionnelle). **Comprendre** ce qui est attendu : répondre à un message écrit (lettre, courriel, post ou article de blog, etc.), transmettre des informations dans un message écrit, demander des informations par écrit... **Repérer** la thématique et le type d'éléments à transmettre.

Astuces

- ***Planifiez*** *votre travail.*
- ***Compensez*** *lorsque le lexique vous manque.*
- ***Recommencez*** *différemment si vous rencontrez des difficultés.*
- ***Corrigez*** *vos maladresses et vos erreurs.*
- ***Respectez*** *les règles du genre (courrier, courriel, article...).*

Noter, rédiger, transmettre lors de votre passage à l'écrit

Préparation

1. **Listez** les éléments à transmettre, les réponses à apporter, les questions à poser.
2. **Notez** vos idées sous forme de mots-clés, de phrases brèves en vous appuyant sur un plan, une carte mentale...
3. **Utilisez** des questions et des réponses connues.
4. **Imitez ou inspirez-vous** d'un modèle connu.

Objectif **Rassembler** vos idées et les **organiser**.

Rédaction du message

5. **Rédigez** les réponses ou les informations à transmettre. **Soyez attentif** au temps, à la grammaire.
6. **Posez** les questions appropriées ; **respectez** l'ordre des mots dans une question.
7. **Utilisez** des expressions adaptées : salutations, formules d'ouverture, de fermeture, demandes polies...

Objectifs **Répondre, transmettre** ou **demander** les éléments attendus. **Respecter** la forme standard du message (lettre, courriel, texto, post, article de blog, discussion en ligne...).

Vérifier votre écrit

1. **Relisez** attentivement votre écrit.
2. **Vérifiez** que vous avez transmis ou demandé l'ensemble des éléments attendus.
3. **Vérifiez** l'orthographe, la grammaire, la ponctuation.

Objectif Vous **autocorriger**.

Useful Words and Sentences, p. 123

Accuracy *la précision*
to achieve *réaliser*
across *à travers, de l'autre côté*
to add *ajouter*
ad/advert/advertisement *une/la publicité*
advice *des conseils*
to advocate *préconiser, promouvoir*
always *toujours*
answering machine *un répondeur*
anthem *un hymne*
apologies *des excuses*
to apply (for) *postuler pour*
• **applicant** *un candidat*
• **application letter** *une lettre de candidature*
appointment *un rendez-vous*
area *un secteur, un quartier*
around *autour de*
astonishing *étonnant*
available *disponible*
average (on) *moyenne (en)*
aware of (to be) *conscient de (être)*

Background *le fond, l'arrière-plan, le contexte*
baker *un boulanger*
balance *l'équilibre*
to ban *interdire*
bank/public holiday *un jour férié*
to begin *commencer*
to behave *se comporter*
• **behaviour** *un comportement*
belief *une croyance*
to belong to *appartenir à*
between *entre*
bold *osé*
bonfire *un feu de joie*
border *une frontière*
to borrow *emprunter*
both *les deux*
break *une pause, une récréation*
to browse *parcourir, rechercher*
BTEC (Business and Technology Education Council) *le baccalauréat professionnel*

Call (to) *appeler*
carbon footprint *l'empreinte carbone*
cardboard *du carton*
care *les soins*
• **caring** *attentionné*
• **carefully** *attentivement*
career exploration fair *un salon des métiers*
to carpool *faire du covoiturage*
catering *la restauration*
chart *un graphique, un tableau*
to cheat *tricher*
to check *vérifier*
chemist's *une pharmacie*
citizen *un citoyen*
classmate *un camarade de classe*
clerk *un employé*
clever *intelligent*
climate change *le changement climatique*
coding *le codage*
to collect *ramasser*
to come (back) *(re)venir*
to commemorate *célébrer*
committed *engagé*
confused *confus*
content *un contenu*
convenient *pratique*
to convert *transformer*
convincing *convaincant*
to count down *compter à rebours*
cover letter *une lettre de motivation*
customer *un client*
cute *adorable*

Day off *un jour de congé*
definitely *absolument*
to design *concevoir*
• **designer** *un styliste*
to destroy *détruire*
to display *afficher, représenter*
district *un quartier*
to download *télécharger, recevoir*
downtown *le centre-ville*
draft *un brouillon*
driven *déterminé*
drought *la sécheresse*
duty *un devoir, une fonction*

Eco-friendly *écologique*
efficient *efficace*
to employ *employer*
• **employer** *un employeur*
• **employee** *un employé*
empty *vide*
to encounter *rencontrer*
energy conservation *les économies d'énergie*
to enjoy *apprécier*
enriching *enrichissant*
entertainment *un divertissement, un loisir*
environmental issues *les questions environnementales*
• **environmentalist** *un écologiste*
exhibition *une exposition*
expat(riate) *un expatrié*

Facilities *les services, les équipements*
to fall *tomber*
feature *une caractéristique*
to feel *sentir*
to find *trouver*
fireworks *un feu d'artifice*
to fit in with *s'intégrer, s'adapter à*
flag *un drapeau*
flight attendant *une hôtesse de l'air / un steward*
flood *une inondation*
folks *les gens*
foreign *étranger*
to found *fonder*
• **founder** *un fondateur*
friend *un ami*
• **friendly** *amical*
full time *à temps plein*

Gateway *un portail*
to get dressed *s'habiller*
to get up *se lever*
global warming *le réchauffement climatique*
goal *un but, un objectif*
GP (general practitioner) *un médecin généraliste*
• **GP surgery** *un cabinet médical*
grateful *reconnaissant*
• **ungrateful** *ingrat*
green *vert, écologique*
• **greenhouse gas** *le gaz à effet de serre*
to greet *saluer*
grocery store *une épicerie*

Half *une moitié, un demi*
hand *une main*
• **hands-on** *pratique, concret*
hardly ever *presque jamais*
hard-working *travailleur*
to harm *nuire*
• **harmful** *nuisible, dangereux*
hazardous *dangereux*
health *la santé*
to hear *entendre*
heart *un cœur*
height *la taille*
to help *aider*
• **helpful** *serviable, pratique*
to highlight *souligner*
to hire *embaucher*
homeless *sans abri*
hospitality *l'accueil*
hour *une heure*
huge *énorme*
to hurt *blesser, faire mal*

ID card *une carte d'identité*
idleness *la paresse, l'oisiveté*
impressed *impressionné*
to improve *améliorer*
income/salary/wages *un salaire*
to increase *augmenter*
information technology (IT) *l'informatique*
insight *un aperçu*
insurance *une assurance*
internship/training period *un stage*
to introduce *présenter*

Join (to) *se joindre à*

Keep (to) *garder*
• **to keep on** *continuer à*
keyword *un mot-clé*
kind *gentil*

WORDS

Landfill *une décharge*
late *tard, en retard*
lazy *fainéant*
to leave a message *laisser un message*
leisure *un loisir*
library *une bibliothèque*
to live *vivre*
• **livability** *l'habitabilité*
• **liveable** *habitable*
• **living being** *un être vivant*
located *situé*
to log in/out *s'identifier/se déconnecter*
to look for *rechercher*
lorry driver *un chauffeur routier*
loud *fort, à haute voix*
lunch break *une pause déjeuner*

Main *principal*
map *une carte*
mechanic *un mécanicien*
to meet *rencontrer*
missing *manquant*
motivated *motivé*
motto *une devise*
museum *un musée*

Narrow *étroit*
to need *avoir besoin*
never *jamais*
noise *le bruit*
• **noisy** *bruyant*

Occupation *un métier*
office *un bureau*
often *souvent*
to open up *s'ouvrir*
opportunity *une occasion, une possibilité*
organic *biologique*
outspoken *franc, spontané*
overcrowded *surpeuplé, bondé*
overtime *des heures supplémentaires*

Packaging *un emballage*
pattern *un motif*
peace *la paix*
• **peaceful** *paisible*
pipe dream *une chimère, un rêve fou*
pleasant *agréable*
to pollute *polluer*
position *un poste*
powerful *puissant*
pretty *joli*
to prevent from *empêcher de*
to promote *promouvoir*
proud *fier*

Queen *une reine*
to quote *citer*

Race *une course*
to range from... to... *varier de... à...*
rarely *rarement*
rate *un taux*
rather than *plutôt que*
to recruit *recruter*
to recycle *recycler*
to reduce *diminuer*
reliable *fiable*
• **unreliable** *peu fiable*
to remember *se souvenir*
renewable *renouvelable*
request *une demande*
• **required** *demandé, exigé*
resource *une ressource*
resume *un CV*
to reuse *réutiliser*
• **reusable** *réutilisable*
to rise *monter, se lever*
rude *grossier*

Safe *sûr, sain*
sales *les ventes, les soldes*
• **salesman** *un vendeur*
to save *économiser*
scam *une fraude, une arnaque*
schedule *un emploi du temps, un planning*
seabed *le fond de la mer*
to search *chercher dans*
• **search engine** *un moteur de recherche*
selfish *égoïste*
sensitive *sensible*
sentence *une phrase*
shape *une forme*
silly *idiot*
single-use *jetable*
size *la taille*
skill *une compétence*
• **skilled worker** *un ouvrier qualifié*
skyscraper *un gratte-ciel*
slum *un quartier pauvre*
smart *élégant, intelligent*
snap *instantané, rapide*
social networks *les réseaux sociaux*
soft *doux*
software *un logiciel*
sometimes *parfois*
to sort out *trier*
to stalk *espionner*
to stand for *signifier, vouloir dire*
to stand up *se lever, se mettre debout*
star *une étoile*
state *un état, un État*
stats/statistics *les statistiques*
steel *l'acier*
store *un magasin*
storm *un orage*
to stroll *se promener*
stubborn *têtu*
strong *fort*
to struggle *se battre*
subject *une discipline, un sujet*
suddenly *soudainement, brusquement*
to summarise/to sum up *résumer*
to surf the Web *naviguer sur Internet*
surgery *une chirurgie, une intervention*
survey *une enquête*
sustainable *durable*
to switch *changer, intervertir*

T
to take a nap *faire la sieste*
talented *talentueux*
to taste *gouter*
to teach *apprendre, enseigner*
team *une équipe*
• **teamwork** *le travail d'équipe*
technician *un technicien*
temporary worker *un intérimaire*
to thank *remercier*
to threaten *menacer*
to throw away *jeter*
tip *un conseil*
tool *un outil*
town hall *une mairie*
traffic *la circulation*
trainee *un stagiaire*
• **training period** *un stage*
to translate *traduire*
travel/journey/trip *un voyage*
the tube *le métro londonien*
to turn on/off *allumer/éteindre*

Ugly *laid*
to understand *comprendre*
unemployment *le chômage*
unfairness *l'injustice*
unpleasant *désagréable*
to upload *télécharger (envoyer)*
to use *utiliser*
• **useful** *utile*
• **useless** *inutile*
• **user-friendly** *facile à utiliser*
usually *habituellement*

Vocational courses *l'enseignement professionnel*

Waiter/waitress *un serveur, une serveuse*
to wake up *se réveiller*
to walk *marcher*
to waste *gaspiller*
• **waste/rubbish/garbage** *des déchets*
to wave *saluer (d'un signe de main)*
wealth *la richesse*
Web designer *un concepteur de site Internet*
to welcome *accueillir*
wide *large*
• **worldwide** *dans le monde entier*
to wish *souhaiter*
to wonder *se demander*
to work out *faire de l'exercice*
to be worth *valoir*

Yet *encore, cependant, toutefois*
youth *la jeunesse*

73 Présenter ou rendre compte d'un support audio, vidéo ou écrit

Type of document

ad/advert/advertisement *une publicité*
broadcast *une émission*
commercial *une publicité télé ou radio*
conversation *une conversation*
detective story *un roman policier*
dialogue *un dialogue*
diary *un journal intime*
documentary *un documentaire*
e-mail *un courriel*
film extract *un extrait de film*
flyer *un prospectus*
instructions for use/operating manual *un mode d'emploi*
interview *un entretien*
job ad/offer *une petite annonce, une offre d'emploi*
leaflet *un dépliant*
letter *une lettre*
mail *un courrier*
message *un message*
news *les informations*
newspaper article *un article de journal*
novel *un roman*
play *une pièce de théâtre*
poem *un poème*
sci-fi *la science-fiction*
speech *un discours*
story *une histoire, un récit*
tale *un conte*
technical document *un document technique*
technical instructions *une notice technique*
thriller *un roman à suspense*
trailer *une bande-annonce*

Information about the document

author *un auteur*
bold letters *des caractères gras*
catch phrase *une accroche, un slogan*
character *un personnage*
date *une date*
figure *une indication chiffrée*
headline *un (gros) titre*
main theme *le thème principal*
monument *un monument*
piece of information *une information*
place *un lieu*
title *un titre*
tone *le ton, la tonalité*

Aim of the document

It aims at... *Il vise à*
to convince *convaincre*
to criticise *critiquer*
to entertain *divertir*
to inform about *informer*
to invent *inventer*
to make aware of *sensibiliser*
to make fun of *se moquer de*
to report *signaler, rapporter*
to take place *se dérouler, avoir lieu*
to tell *raconter*

74 S'exprimer à l'oral ou à l'écrit

Organising your speech

I'm going to talk about... *Je vais parler de...*
Today, I would like to speak about... *Aujourd'hui, j'aimerais parler de...*
I've chosen to speak about... *J'ai choisi de parler de...*
M. X says / thinks that... *M. X dit / pense que...*
First of all, I will/I'm going to explain/ to describe... *Tout d'abord, j'expliquerai/ je vais décrire...*
Then, I will move onto... *Ensuite, je parlerai de...*
And finally, I will give my opinion about... *Pour conclure, je donnerai mon avis sur...*

Justifying

The reason why... *La raison pour laquelle...*
Let me explain... *Laissez-moi vous expliquer...*
For example... *Par exemple...*
Take the example of... *Prenez l'exemple de...*
It means that... *Cela veut dire que...*

Summing up and concluding

In short/To sum up... *En résumé...*
In general (terms)... *En général...*
actually *en fait, à vrai dire*
that is to say *c'est-à-dire*
all in all *en somme, tout compte fait*
To conclude/As a conclusion... *Pour conclure...*
(I would like to) thank you for your attention. *Je vous remercie pour votre attention.*

75 Interagir à l'écrit et à l'oral

Layout

enclosure/attached document *une pièce jointe*
recipient *un destinataire*
signature *une signature*

Formal greeting and closing formula

- **Dear Sir / Madam / Mr X / Mrs X**
- **Yours faithfully / Yours sincerely / With best wishes**

Informal greeting and closing formula

- **Hi Tim, / Dear Jane, / Hi there, / Hello, / Hi everyone,**
- **Sincerely. / Regards. / Kind regards. / Thank you. / Warm wishes. / Many thanks. / Cheers, John**
- **Love from... / Speak soon! / XoXoXX**

Formal expressions

I am writing to thank you for... *Je vous écris pour vous remercier de...*
I look forward to seeing you next week. *J'attends avec impatience de vous voir la semaine prochaine.*

Informal expressions

Many thanks for your help. *Merci pour ton aide.*
See you next week! *À la semaine prochaine !*

On the phone

Good morning. This is (+ name)... *Bonjour. C'est (+ nom)...*
You can call me (back) at... *Vous pouvez m'appeler (me rappeler) au...*
Thanks in advance for returning my call. *Je vous remercie par avance de me rappeler.*
Can you deliver a message for me, please? *Pouvez-vous transmettre un message de ma part, s'il vous plait ?*

RECAP

WORDS AND SENTENCES

Auxiliary *Be* – Unit 1, Challenge 4, p. 11

To be (être) est le seul verbe qui ait trois formes différentes au présent (*am, are, is*) et deux formes différentes au prétérit (*was* au singulier et *were* au pluriel).

Dans la langue parlée, *I am* devient *I'm*, *you are* devient *you're* et *he is* devient *he's*.

Pour poser une question, on inverse l'auxiliaire et le sujet : *Are you confused?*

On utilise toujours *to be* au prétérit pour donner des précisions sur sa naissance : *I was born in November.*

	Présent	Prétérit	Futur
I	am	was	will be
You	are	were	
He/She/It	is	was	
We You They	are	were	

Questions with *How* – Unit 1, Challenge 2, p. 11

How est très souvent utilisé comme mot interrogatif, par exemple pour demander « Comment ça va ? » : *How are you?*

Il peut être enrichi d'un adjectif ou d'un adverbe (*old, tall, far...*).

Cet adjectif ou adverbe est généralement repris dans la réponse : *How tall are you? I'm 1.80 metres tall.*

Pour demander **l'âge :** *How old?*
Pour demander **la taille :** *How tall?*
Pour demander **la distance :** *How far?*

How many? – Unit 1, Challenge 2, p. 13

Pour interroger sur une quantité dénombrable (ce qui peut se compter), on utilise le pronom interrogatif *How many?*.

Pour dire « il y a », on utilise *there is* devant un nom au singulier et *there are* devant un nom au pluriel.

À la forme interrogative, on inverse le sujet et l'auxiliaire : *are there/is there?*

How many inhabitants are there in London? **There are** nine million inhabitants in London.

What Time? – Unit 1, Challenge 2, p. 15

Pour répondre à la question *What time is it?* et indiquer l'heure :

- on indique d'abord les minutes ;
- on ajoute ensuite « *past* » lorsque l'on est dans la première demi-heure **ou** « *to* » lorsque l'on est dans la seconde demi-heure ;
- on précise enfin l'heure indiquée par la petite aiguille.

Les expressions « et quart » et « moins le quart » se disent *a quarter past* et *a quarter to* ; « et demi » se dit *half past*.

Pour les heures piles, on ajoute *o'clock* derrière le nombre d'heures.

On fait suivre les heures par les lettres *a.m.* (avant-midi) ou *p.m.* (après-midi).

Pour indiquer les horaires de début et de fin d'une activité, on utilise les prépositions *from* et *to* (de... à...).

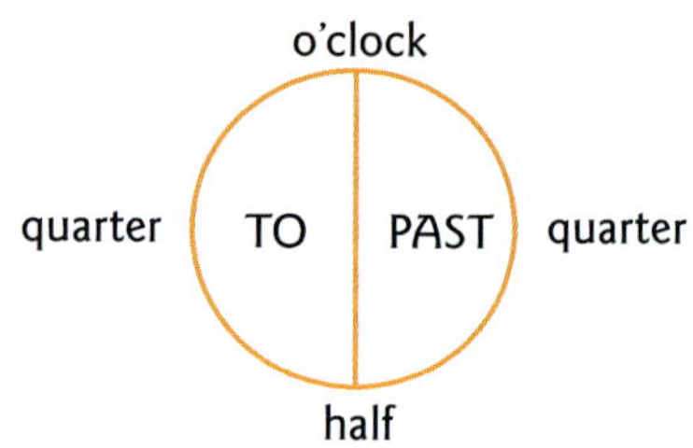

Daily Routine – Unit 2, Challenge 2, p. 25

On utilise le présent simple pour exprimer une habitude.

- **À la forme affirmative :** *I/You/We/They* + BV
He/She/It + *-s* **ou** *-es* pour les verbes qui se terminent par « *-s* », « *-z* », « *-x* », « *-sh* », « *-ch* » et « *-o* ».
- **À la forme négative :** *I/You/We/They* + *don't* + BV **ou** *He/She/It* + *doesn't* + BV

1. Elon **sleeps** for just six hours.
2. He **doesn't** really **have** breakfast.
3. I always **get up** at 6.30 a.m.

Adjectives: Position in Sentences – Unit 2, Challenge 2, p. 27

- **Les adjectifs épithètes** se placent devant le nom qu'ils qualifient.

Quand il y a plusieurs adjectifs devant un nom, ils sont placés du plus subjectif au plus objectif : jugement personnel, puis information sur la taille, l'âge, la couleur, l'origine, la matière.

- **Les adjectifs attributs** se placent après un verbe d'état (*be, seem, look...*).

1. Zendaya is a **fabulous 23-year-old American** actress.
2. Malala Yousafzai is **brave** and **intelligent**.

Simple Present/Questions – Unit 3, Challenge 2, p. 37

• Pour une question fermée au présent simple (réponse attendue : oui/non), on utilise l'auxiliaire *do* à toutes les personnes ou *does* à la 3e personne du singulier : → Auxiliaire + sujet + BV?

Réponse brève : *Yes*, sujet + *do/does* ou *No*, sujet + *don't/doesn't*.

• Pour les questions ouvertes au présent simple (réponse attendue : une information), on ajoute un mot interrogatif en début de question.

1. **Does** she **like** tea? Yes, she **does**.
2. What sports **do** you **practise**? I **practice** skateboarding and surfing.

Comparisons – Unit 3, Challenge 2, p. 39

Pour comparer deux éléments entre eux, on utilise le comparatif de supériorité :

• **adjectifs courts** (1 syllabe), on rajoute *-er* à l'adjectif ;

• **adjectifs longs** (2 syllabes et plus), on ajoute *more* avant l'adjectif.

Dans les deux cas, on utilise *than* pour introduire le 2d élément de comparaison (s'il est présent).

Attention : les adjectifs finissant par « *-y* » se transforment en « *-ier* » : *crazy* → *crazier*.

Les adjectifs irréguliers : *good* → *better* ; *bad* → *worse*.

1. You are tall**er than** your cousin.
tall → taller
2. Your brother is **more** dynamic **than** your best friend.
dynamic → more dynamic

Superlatives – Unit 3, Challenge 2, p. 41

Pour comparer quelqu'un/quelque chose à un ensemble de personnes/de choses, on utilise le superlatif :

• **adjectifs courts :** *the* + adjectif + *-est ;*

• **adjectifs longs :** *the* + *most* + adjectif.

Attention : les adjectifs se terminant par « *-y* » se transforment en « *-iest* » : *easy* → *easiest*.

Adjectifs irréguliers : *good* → *the best* ; *bad* → *the worst*.

1. Do you know **the** fast**est** runner in the world?
fast → the fastest
2. She is **the most** courageous athlete of her team.
courageous → the most courageous

Obligation – Unit 4, Challenge 2, p. 51

Pour exprimer une obligation, on utilise le modal *must*.

Il se place entre le sujet et la base verbale.

Pour exprimer une interdiction, on utilise *mustn't*.

1. You **must** be 18 to vote in France.
2. You **mustn't** smoke in the classroom.

"The" or "Ø"? – Unit 4, Challenge 2, p. 53

• On utilise l'article « *the* » pour désigner une personne, un objet, un évènement précis et défini.

• Quand un nom représente une notion abstraite ou une généralité, on supprime cet article. On dit qu'on utilise l'article zéro.

1. I like **the** colour blue.
2. I'm crazy about chocolate.

Simple Past – Unit 5, Challenge 2, p. 63

Lorsqu'une action est passée, datée et terminée, on utilise le prétérit.

• **Forme affirmative :** BV + *-ed* **ou** verbe irrégulier (voir **FLAP** 2e colonne de la liste des verbes irréguliers).

• ***To be* au prétérit :** *I was / You were / He - she - it was / We were / You were / They were.*

In 1776, the Congress **adopted** the Declaration of Independence. This **was** the birth of the United States

Giving Dates – Unit 5, Challenge 2, p. 65

Pour introduire une date, on ajoute la préposition :

• *in* pour indiquer une année ;

• *in* pour indiquer un mois ;

• *on* pour indiquer un jour précis.

In 2022 / **In** September / **On** the 4th of July...

Relative Pronouns *who* and *which* – Unit 5, Challenge 2, p. 67

Lorsque deux phrases sont reliées pour former un seul énoncé, on utilise le pronom relatif :

• *who* pour une personne ;

• *which* pour un objet ou un concept.

1. The election **which** took place in 1994 in South Africa was the first democratic one.
2. Nelson Mandela, **who** was the first black president, is still the symbol of freedom in South Africa.

RECAP

Goals - Unit 6, Challenge 2, p. 77

- Pour exprimer le but, on utilise *to* ou *in order to*.
- Pour poser une question sur le but, on peut dire « *What is the aim?* » ou encore « *What is the purpose?* ».

Attention : contrairement au français, on ne peut jamais utiliser « *for* » pour exprimer le but.

The Victorian Government is working **to/in order to** improve livability.

Future - Unit 6, Challenge 2, p. 79

Pour exprimer une action future, une prédiction, on utilise l'auxiliaire *will*.

- **À la forme affirmative :** S + *will* + BV.
- **À la forme négative :** S + *won't* + BV.

NB : *will not = won't / 'll = will.*

1. You **will** spend less money.
2. You **won't** waste energy.

Recommendations - Unit 7, Challenge 2, p. 89

Pour donner un ordre, recommander ou suggérer fortement, on utilise **l'impératif**.

- **À la forme affirmative :** BV !
- **À la forme négative :** *Don't* + BV !

1. Please, **eat** less meat!
2. Please, **don't eat** too much meat!

Need to - Unit 7, Challenge 4, p. 89

Pour exprimer la nécessité (il faut que), on emploie *need to*, suivi d'une base verbale.

You **need to** eat less meat to protect the environment.

Conditions - Unit 7, Challenge 2, p. 91

Pour exprimer une condition ou une hypothèse, on utilise :
S + *will/won't* + BV... ***if*** + S + BV.

NB : si les éléments sont inversés, une virgule sépare les deux propositions.

You **will** get fertiliser for free **if** you **compost** your kitchen waste.

Don't Have to - Unit 7, Challenge 2, p. 93

On utilise *don't have to* pour exprimer l'absence d'obligation (ne pas avoir besoin de...) : S + *don't/doesn't have to* + BV.

We **don't have to** sacrifice environment to get a strong economy.

What: Relative Pronoun or Question Word? - Unit 8, Challenge 2, p. 103

- *What* peut être un pronom interrogatif (que... ? quel... ? quoi... ?) pour former une question : *What* + auxiliaire + sujet + BV ?
- *What* peut également être un pronom relatif (que, ce que) dans une phrase affirmative ou négative : *what* + sujet + BV.

1. **What** do you prefer in this app?
2. **What** we like is that we can add commentaries.

Adverbs Ending with *-ly* - Unit 8, Challenge 2, p. 105

- Les adverbes peuvent être construits à partir d'adjectifs. Dans ce cas, on leur ajoute généralement la terminaison *-ly*.
- L'adverbe est invariable et est généralement placé avant le verbe ou après l'auxiliaire « être ».

1. I **clearly** prefer this app.
2. This app is **simply** an online planner.

♪ WORDS AND SOUNDS

Wh- or Yes/No Questions – Unit 1, Challenge 3, p. 11

Wh- questions : intonation descendante ↘.
Yes/No questions : intonation montante ↗.

Saying Nationalities – Unit 1, Challenge 3, p. 13

Mots	Syllabe accentuée	Exemples
2 syllabes	première	**Eng**lish, **Spa**nish, **I**rish…
Terminés par *-ese*	dernière	Chi**nese**, Japa**nese**, Portu**guese**…
Terminés par *-ian*	avant-dernière	**In**dian, Ca**na**dian, Aus**tra**lian…

The Sound [h] – Unit 1, Challenge 3, p. 15

Règle générale : le « h » se prononce en début de mot : *hello, hi, happy, how, half…*

Quelques exceptions : *hour, honest, honour…*

Ne pas confondre : *hand / and ; hair / air…*

The Letter "s" at the End of a Verb – Unit 2, Challenge 3, p. 25

Le « *-s* » qui marque la 3e personne du singulier au présent simple se prononce :

- /s/ après une consonne « sourde » (p, t, k et f) : *he stops / he eats* ;
- /z/ après une voyelle ou une consonne « sonore » (b, d, g, m, l, n, v…) : *he goes / he finds* ;
- /iz/ après un son « sifflant » (/dʒ/, /s/, /z/, /ʃ/, /tʃ/) : *he kisses / he buzzes.*

Words Ending with *-er* – Unit 3, Challenge 3, p. 39

La terminaison *-er* des mots se prononce /ə/, comme dans *player*.

On dit qu'il s'agit d'un son faible. C'est le son le plus fréquent en anglais britannique.

The Letter "o" – Unit 3, Challenge 3, p. 41

La lettre « o » peut se prononcer :

- /ɔ:/ comme dans *short* ;
- /ɒ/ comme dans *top* ;
- /əu/ comme dans *broken.*

The Letter "y" – Unit 4, Challenge 3, p. 51

La lettre « y » peut se prononcer :

- /aı/ comme dans *type* ;
- /i/ comme dans *typical.*

Ou dans des sons composés :

- /eı/ comme dans *day* ;
- /ɔı/ comme dans *employ.*

-ed Pronunciation – Unit 5, Challenge 3, p. 63

Le « *-ed* » du prétérit se prononce de 3 manières : /t/ **ou** /d/ **ou** /id/.

Attention : il ne se prononce **jamais** /ed/.

- Si « *-ed* » est précédé de la lettre « t » ou « d », il se prononcera /id/ : *wanted* ; *added.*
- Si c'est une autre lettre, il se prononcera /t/ ou /d/ : *looked* ; *signed.*

The Letter "i" – Unit 6, Challenge 3, p. 77

La lettre « i » peut se prononcer :

- /aı/ comme dans *diverse* ;
- /i/ comme dans *facilities* ;
- elle peut également être neutre comme dans la 3e syllabe de *communities* et *facilities* : /ə/.

Remarque : l'ajout d'un « *-e* » final change la prononciation de la lettre « i » : *kit /i/ vs kite/aı/ ; trip /i/ vs tripe /aı/.*

Silent Letters – Unit 6, Challenge 3, p. 79

Certaines consonnes sont muettes :

- la lettre « b » dans *climb, doubt, bomb, debt…* ;
- la lettre « k » dans *know, knock, knife, knee…* ;
- la lettre « w » dans *answer, two, sword, wrap…* ;
- la letter « h » dans *mechanic, hour, school, what…*

/i/ vs /i:/ – Unit 7, Challenge 3, p. 89

Le son « i » peut correspondre à 2 prononciations : /i/ ou /i:/.

Le son /i:/ peut correspondre à différentes graphies :

- « ea » comme dans *meat* ;
- « ee » comme dans *need* ;
- « ie » comme dans *field* ;
- « ei » comme dans *ceiling* ;
- « eo » comme dans *people* ;
- « i » comme dans *machine.*

Want or *won't*? – Unit 7, Challenge 3, p. 91

- *Want* → /wɑnt/ → verbe vouloir : un seul son voyelle.
- *Won't* → /wəʊnt/ → contraction de *will* + *not* : un double son voyelle (ou diphtongue).

The Letter "a" – Unit 7, Challenge 3, p. 93

La lettre « a » peut se prononcer de plusieurs façons :

- /ei/ comme dans *bacon* ;
- /æ/ comme dans *man* ;
- /e/ comme dans *many* ;
- /i/ comme dans *message* ;
- /ɑ:/ comme dans *car* ;
- /əe/ comme dans *care* ;
- /ɒ/ comme dans *watch* ;
- /ɔ:/ comme dans *talk.*
- /ə/ comme dans *arrival* ;

The Letter "u" – Unit 8, Challenge 3, p. 103

La lettre « u » peut se prononcer :

- /ʌ/ comme dans *fun* ;
- /ju/ comme dans *communication* ;
- /u:/ comme dans *intrusive* ;
- /v/ comme dans *two.*

CRÉDITS PHOTOS

Couverture et p. 8, 9, 12, 16, 19, 22, 32, 36, 44, 45, 48, 54, 56, 60, 61 (b), 66, 68, 70, 71, 72 (b), 73, 74, 80 (h, m), 84, 87, 90, 94, 95, 96, 97, 100, 101, 113 : © AdobeStock - **p. 23 :** © www.isd728.org / dr - **p. 24 :** UPI/ABACA - **p. 26 :** OConnor Lisa/AFF/ABACA ; Philpott Hugo/UPI/ABACA ; SIPANY/SIPA - **p. 28 :** zz/RE/Westcom/STAR MAX/IPx/AP/SIPA - **p. 31 :** Kevin Mazur / Getty Images - **p. 34 :** NIVIERE/SIPA - **p. 35 :** © olympic.org - **p. 40 :** OIS/Jed Leicester/REX/SIPA - **p. 49 :** © Shutterstock - **p. 61 (h) :** © Boyko.Pictures/Shutterstock - **p. 64 :** Lenscap / Alamy / Hemis - **p. 72 (hg) :** Photo © AGIP / Bridgeman Images - **p. 78 :** © OCEANIX/BIG-Bjarke Ingels Group - **p. 80 :** © Shutterstock - **p. 83 :** Nathaniel Noir / Alamy / Hemis - **p. 86 :** © Sudarsan Pattnaik - **p. 92 :** © Ocean Club, www.4ocean.com - **p. 112 :** © Warner Bros / Village Roadshow Pictures

Création couverture, conception maquette, illustrations : Séverine Tanguy

Mise en page : Séverine Tanguy, assistée de Nadine Aymard

Édition et iconographie : Annabelle Biau-Weber

Relecture : Estelle Jelen

Exercices interactifs : Desk

Enregistrements audio : Studio Eurodvd

Dépôt légal: mars 2021 – N° éditeur: MAGSI20200719
Achevé d'imprimer en mars 2021 par Bona SpA en Italie

PEFC/18-31-407